Project and Programme Accounting

A practical guide for professional services organisations and IT

Project and Programme Accounting

A practical guide for professional services organisations and IT

John Chapman

Project Manager Today
PUBLICATIONS

Project Manager Today Publications
Larchdrift Projects Ltd, Unit 12, Moor Place Farm, Plough Lane, Bramshill, Hook, Hampshire RG27 0RF

First published in Great Britain 2006

© John Chapman

The right of John Chapman to be identified as author of this work has been asserted in accordance with the Copyright, Designs and Patents Act 1988.

ISBN: 1-900391-14-7

British Library Cataloguing in Publication Data

Chapman, John
   Project and programme accounting : a practical guide for professional services organisations and IT
   1.Cost accounting 2.Program budgeting 3.Project management
   I.Title
   657.4'2

ISBN-10: 1900391147

All rights reserved; no part of this publication may be reproduced, stored in a retrieval system, or transmitted in any form or by any means, electronic, mechanical, photocopying, recording, or otherwise without the prior permission of the publishers. This book may not be lent, resold, hired out or otherwise disposed of by way of trade in any form or binding or cover other than that which it is published, without the consent of the publishers.

The book is published on the understanding that the author is solely responsible for the statements made and opinions expressed in it and that its publication does not necessarily imply that such statements and/or opinions are or reflect the views or opinions of the publishers.

Printed and bound in Great Britain by Biddles Limited

Acknowledgements

I am extremely grateful for all the support and assistance I have been given in preparing this book. The individuals named below have been of particular assistance and I thank them.

Keith Birch, Chief Executive, Touchstone Group PLC, for his support and advice on looking for additional sources to test my theories, my reasoning and the applicability of ideas contained herein.

Geoff Reiss, PM Group plc, and author of a number of books including *Programme Management Demystified*, for his encouragement, ideas and advice on how to write and publish a book.

Peter Court, Programme Manager, Office of Government Commerce, for reviewing the manuscript, and providing suggestions on how I could improve the content.

Dr Liz Bacon, Head of School, Computing and Mathematical Sciences, University of Greenwich, for reviewing the manuscript, and providing support to me on promoting the book.

In addition, I received input, advice and assistance from Malcolm Anthony, David Birch, Chris Butler, Damian Edwards, Phil Harwood, Graham James, Rob Jones, Richard Long, David Marsh, Adrian Morrish, Peter Mystris, Sarah Perkins, Adrian Pyne, Paul Rayner, Tom Saunders, Szto You Koong, Tony Teague and Paul White, all of whom I thank.

In closing, two people need particular mention:

Ken Lane, Editorial Director of Project Manager Today Publications, for proofreading my manuscript, giving helpful advice and publishing this book.

Most importantly, to my wife Sarah for her understanding, during the many hours I sat writing and updating the manuscript.

Foreword

I have spent some 25 years in project and programme management and have watched sadly as successive generations of project and programme managers have either lacked the ability or, more likely, the desire, to control the 'financials' of their change initiatives properly.

There are glaring examples of public-sector disasters but, be assured, there are even more in the private sector. So why haven't those in charge of governance of these programmes taken heed of the early warning signs produced by their management systems so that proper control could be exercised?

The answer is that, on all too many occasions, programme and project managers abandon their responsibilities for financial control. They leave 'the detail to the accountancy department to deal with'. Unfortunately, as an accountant, I believe the accountancy profession is woefully inexperienced and often not qualified to establish the type of financial monitoring and control systems required to effectively manage business-change programmes.

So, we have two professions that rely on each other, where neither is capable nor interested enough to handle it on their own.

It is clear that the programme and project management profession must take the lead and the accountancy profession provide the service.

John Chapman is one project director who was not prepared to sit on his hands and allow these problems to persist. He set about his financial control duties the hard way by understanding the requirement, designing a solution, and building and implementing a system of programme and project accounting that works, and deals with benefits as well as costs!

He does not want anyone else to go through his pain; so he has written this practical book to get project and programme people and accountants to benefit from his experience. One of our challenges it to get people to take these issues seriously. This is one of the first books to do so.

You will find that this book has been written in a way that enables both the experienced and inexperienced to chart different routes through it, so expanding its potential influence. Please enjoy it, benefit from it, and spread the word among your fellow professionals that financial control of projects and programmes is often the difference between success and failure.

Graham James
Director, SGA Business Consulting Ltd

Preface

Working as Project Director for a company who deliver systems, I needed to understand the issues around project and programme accounting. However, I was unable to find a single source of information on what was required for a professional services business. Furthermore, for organisations that have an internal IT function, there was no reference material available for the identification of programme and project costs.

So I wrote this book to help others understand this vital subject. It also explains how a system can be implemented to deliver strong reporting both on individual projects and programmes as well as across the organisation as a whole. Reporting the cost of the programme or project in areas where there are specific overruns or under-runs helps management effort to be focused on improving overall effectiveness and efficiency.

My own introduction to programme management was from Geoff Reiss's book, *Programme Management Demystified*. After reading his book I introduced programme management to Touchstone (www.touchstone.co.uk), both in the delivery of programmes of business change and as an operational mechanism for managing multiple projects with multiple customers.

Successful project and programme management is essential for any organisation. I was involved in the development of the OGC's *Managing Successful Programmes* (1st Edition) and this has since been joined by training and qualifications in MSP.

I hope that this book will mean that other people do not have the frustration I felt when trying to find the information to set up practical systems.

John Chapman

Where should I start?

If you are new to project and programme accounting then I suggest you read Section 1 first, and then progress through the rest of the book. However, if you have an understanding of revenue and cost management, know about cash collection and payment, and resource planning, then you will probably find Section 1 too basic. I suggest you skim through the headings in each chapter and read the 'Design basics' before moving on to Section 2, 'Advanced design concepts'.

If you want to implement a system, and have a good understanding of the issues, then read Section 4. The chapter on 'Implementing a system' will give you guidance on how to approach the problem. The chapter on software requirements will assist in preparing a requirements specification to issue to software vendors.

For those of you who do not work in an organisation which charges customers for their time, then Chapter 5 – 'Receivables or sales ledger' – is likely to be of academic interest only. Furthermore, if you do not have to worry about cash, as this is dealt with by another part of the business, then Chapter 7 – 'Cash' – can be skipped.

Contents

v Acknowledgements
vii Foreword
ix Preface
xi Where should I start?

1 SECTION 1: BASIC INTRODUCTION
Topics include the benefits of implementing a system, designing a system, budgeting, income (receivables), and expenditure (payables), cash and resource planning.

1 Introduction
An introduction to project and programme accounting, identifying the differences from financial accounting. Programme management is introduced, looking at portfolio project management using programme management and change programmes.

8 Benefits
The benefits that can be derived from implementing a comprehensive project and programme accounting system.

15 Design basics
Data sources. A model for a project and programme accounting system.

28 Budgets
Company versus programme budgets. How is a programme or project budget made up? Converting time into money, budgeting for expenses and how to handle contingency and tolerance.

46 Receivables or sales ledger
Raising invoices, getting paid, revenue recognition and credit notes. Introduction to the general ledger and how mappings are made from one system to another.

59 Payables/purchase ledger
Controlling and analysing purchases for a project or programme.

64 Cash
Cash-flow forecasting, improving cash management, using Microsoft Project to produce a cash-flow forecast.

69 Resource planning & utilisation
Calculating working days in the year, productive days and resource planning.

75 Time recording
Implementing a timesheet culture.

85 Expenses
Recording expenses, expense analysis.

91 SECTION 2: ADVANCED CONCEPTS
Project and programme hierarchies, working with employees and skills, sample design ideas for different organisations. Change control and the impact of contract terms on project and programme accounting.

91 Advanced design concepts
Nested hierarchies, employees, and their relationship in the entity relationship model.

102 Change control
Change control in the context of a project or programme accounting system.

105 Contract terms
Introduction to contract terms and their effect on the project or programme cost and revenue schedules.

107 Resource planning & utilisation examples
Resource planning for a consultancy business is considered and extended to look at the business life cycle and how it affects the planning of work.

123 SECTION 3: REPORTING
Reporting and types of reports that you should be getting from a system.

123 Analysing the data
Reporting is split between operational improvements and strategic improvements.

131 SECTION 4: DEFINING AND IMPLEMENTING A SYSTEM
Guidance on how to implement a project or programme accounting system (irrespective of the package you choose). Sample list of the type of requirements you should be looking for from a packaged solution.

131 Implementation issues
Where do you start? A list of things to do to ensure a successful implementation.

145 Software requirements
Where do you start and what do you look for in software?

176 Conclusion

177 SECTION 5: ADDITIONAL READING
177 Bibliography
177 Contacts

179 Index

Section One: Introduction

I often say that when you can measure what you are speaking about, and express it in numbers, you know something about it; but when you cannot measure it, when you cannot express it in numbers, your knowledge is of a meagre and unsatisfactory kind. It may be the beginning of knowledge, but you have scarcely in your thoughts advanced to the state of science, whatever the matter may be.

Lord Kelvin

WHY PROJECT AND PROGRAMME ACCOUNTING?

The pace of change in business is going even faster and, to counter this threat, a business needs to develop new offerings (products and/or services) and improve the competitiveness of its existing portfolio.

As margins are squeezed, and the drive for shareholder value increases, the justification of particular lines of businesses becomes more critical.

A new service or product forms part of an internal programme or project. Return on investment (ROI) will be vitally important and can only be determined if you know the cost of development and the subsequent revenues realised.

Similar pressures exist in internal IT departments where budgets are under threat to justify millions of pounds of expenditure. Without ways of tracking costs, boards of directors cannot see if they are getting value for money.

Public-sector organisations face a similar challenge in justifying expenditure. The delivery of change management will require an analysis of the time and cost incurred. Using project and programme accounting techniques, it will be possible to report this information.

In a project- or programme-based business, it is important to report on and analyse costs and revenue by project and programme.

Traditional accounting versus projects and programmes

Accounting systems are not set up to work in project or programme terms. Table A overleaf illustrates the important differences.

Furthermore, there are other issues that impact on the business, but are not necessarily aligned to projects or programmes. For example, see Table B overleaf.

By understanding the accounting issues, you can design a solution that will meet the reporting needs of both the project or programme, and the business.

Job costing and contract costing

The methods of job costing and contract costing in cost and management accounting go some way to address the requirements for project and programme accounting. However, they are nowhere nearly sophisticated enough to meet the requirements of the world of business change management.

Traditional accounting	Projects & programmes
Companies report in financial periods based on a financial year.	Projects and programmes have start dates, deliverable dates and end dates which are unlikely to relate to any concept of accounting periods.
Accounting departments produce figures on an accounting period basis, whether that is monthly (12 periods per year), every 4 weeks (13 periods per year), weekly (52 periods), or daily (365 periods.)	Project and programme reporting will be aligned to deliverable and activity. This is unlikely to be based on fixed accounting periods linked to the annual calendar.
Accounts reporting is based on a hierarchy of departments and cost centres.	Projects and programmes cover many departments and cost centres.
Financial and management reporting is likely to be country-based and dependent on the statutory requirements of that country.	Projects and programmes can be international, covering many different statutory accounting requirements. An IT department will need to be able to report in a common format, so it will need to define a system which sits alongside the financial and management accounting.
Customers are the key to sales revenue analysis, not project or programme.	If programme management is being used to run multiple projects across multiple customers, then it is necessary to link by type of project or programme, not by customer.
Comparative reporting is based on same period last year and actual versus budget.	Projects and programmes can only be compared if their characteristics are similar.
Public-sector organisations budget by financial year, as this is in line with the money voted by Parliament in the Budget.	The project and programme could cross one or more financial years.

Table A

Types of project

What is a project? In setting up a project and programme accounting system, this is a serious question that needs to be answered.

Typically, there will be different project types, and projects will fall into classifications. The projects and programmes themselves will have different characteristics depending on whether they are:

Other issues	Stakeholder considerations
In a public limited company the pressure is on to deliver results every 6 months.	The project or programme, unless designed to deliver results with your organisations accounting periods in mind, will find itself at odds with senior management in producing revenue.
Cash is king. The Accounts Department has a credit controller who will chase invoices.	Project or programme managers will want to manage the relationship and are unlikely to want outside people ringing up demanding payment.
Project and programme completion, and keeping in budget	How many projects or programmes have been run which are almost completed? As the end date comes close, a large amount of resource is suddenly thrown at the project to ensure completion. The budget is ignored as the drive for completion gathers momentum. Go-live is achieved, everyone is congratulated and the overrun is ignored – swept under the table as new projects and programmes start up.

Table B

- part of an internal IT department
- for an IT or professional services business which charges for the work.

Internal IT department
The internal IT department could consider projects as types of work. These would fall into different classifications, such as building new PCs and servers, working on new implementations (each of which is treated as a project in its own right), or providing help-desk support to existing systems

IT or professional services business
In an IT or professional services business, there will be a number of different project and programme types. Projects could cover training, design, requirements analysis as individual projects, or combined together for a total solution. These would be charged to different customers.

A definition of the project in an organisation is needed to create the requisite entries in the project and programme accounting system. Attributes to look for are: the start date, the end date, the deliverables, the activities and the project manager. Clearly these are needed. Trying to break down the activities into component parts, where this has not been performed before, can be a challenge.

The start point for the system is a strong design. This can be refined as time progresses, but 'What constitutes a project?' needs to be thought through in the first instance.

Types of programmes

During the development of the OGC's *Managing Successful Programmes* guidelines, there was considerable discussion on 'What is a programme?'. You need to define what constitutes a programme or a project in the context of your business.

In the early stages of implementing a project and programme culture, defining a project or programme may appear simple but will require much forethought. Later, in the design chapter, I have outlined a hierarchical relationship from activity up to programme.

The important point is, however programmes and projects are defined, there must be consistency across projects and programmes to ensure that valuable analysis can be produced. The project and programme structure will then need to be mapped to the company's accounting system.

Runners, repeaters and strangers

In *Programme Management Demystified*, projects are classified in three groups: runners, repeaters and strangers.

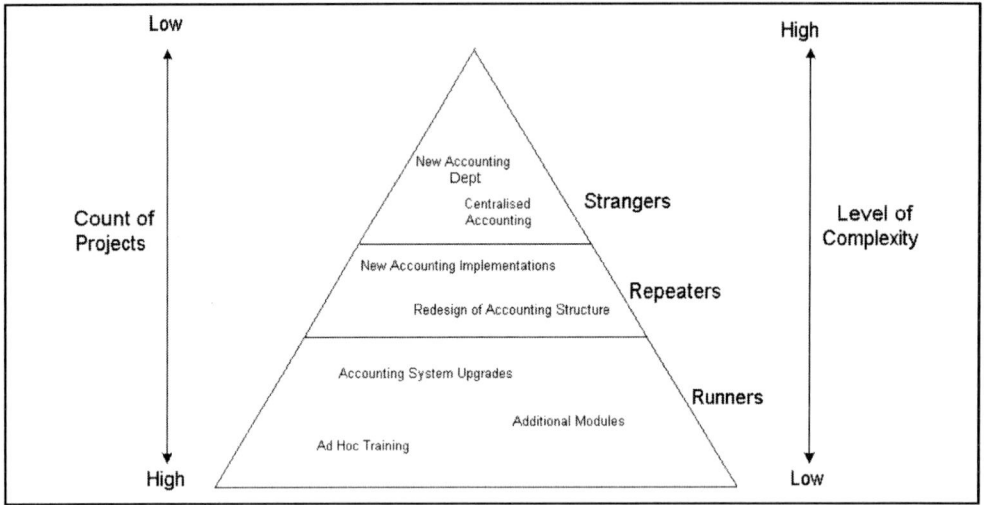

Runners

Runners are projects that the organisation performs frequently. In the case of an accounting services provider, this would cover ad hoc consultancy, software upgrades (from one release to another), implementation of additional software modules (fixed assets, purchase invoice register), and so forth.

For IT departments, there are likely to be similar project types, such as upgrades to operating systems and office automation software, building replacement servers and PCs, and other like items.

Repeaters

Repeaters are projects that the organisation performs with less frequency than runners, but more than strangers. For an accounting services provider this would cover, for instance, new implementations of systems, major redesign of an accounting system, detailed technical consultancy and so forth.

An internal IT department might see repeaters in the form of new projects implemented by different departments in the business. For example, a document management system for a company's tax department could be duplicated in the company secretary's department.

Strangers

Strangers are projects that the organisation performs infrequently. An example might be a major change project such as the consolidation of accounting centres to one site. Alternatively, this could be the delivery of strategic initiatives or one-off projects, such as setting up a new distribution centre.

Advantages

There are clear advantages to dividing the work into these groupings of projects:

1. The development of standard work packages allows a consistent approach.
   For an internal IT department, this would assist in planning workloads. For a company who charge for work, a consistent approach can be developed from sales presentation through to system delivery.
2. The 'productising' of runners, repeaters and strangers reduces the time to deliver the project, which would make the organisation more competitive
3. By delivering pre-defined, known pieces of work, it is possible to look at non-conformance in a more consistent manner.
4. Because the type of work performed is identifiable, training and development needs can be matched to projects and programmes.

The first step in developing a project and programme reporting culture is to treat these three distinct groups (runners/repeaters/strangers) as programmes in their own right. Each starts at the beginning of a financial year and runs to the end of the financial year. Within the repeater programme, for example, there is a sub-programme, which is the accounting implementation programme and all the projects under it are analysed in the context of the programme.

In this, the first step, you are trying to align accounting periods with the analysis of projects and programmes. The projects in a programme may well cover more than one financial year. The financial year is used to give comparative analysis on effectiveness.

The questions to ask:

- What are the different services (which become projects) do you offer? (Internal departments as well as customer-charging organisations both offer services to their respective groups.)

- Can you list the types of projects that you run at present? (Remember it is the type of project you are interest in.)
- How would they fit into the above pyramid?

Change programmes

A change programme moves the business from one blueprint to another, represented schematically as:

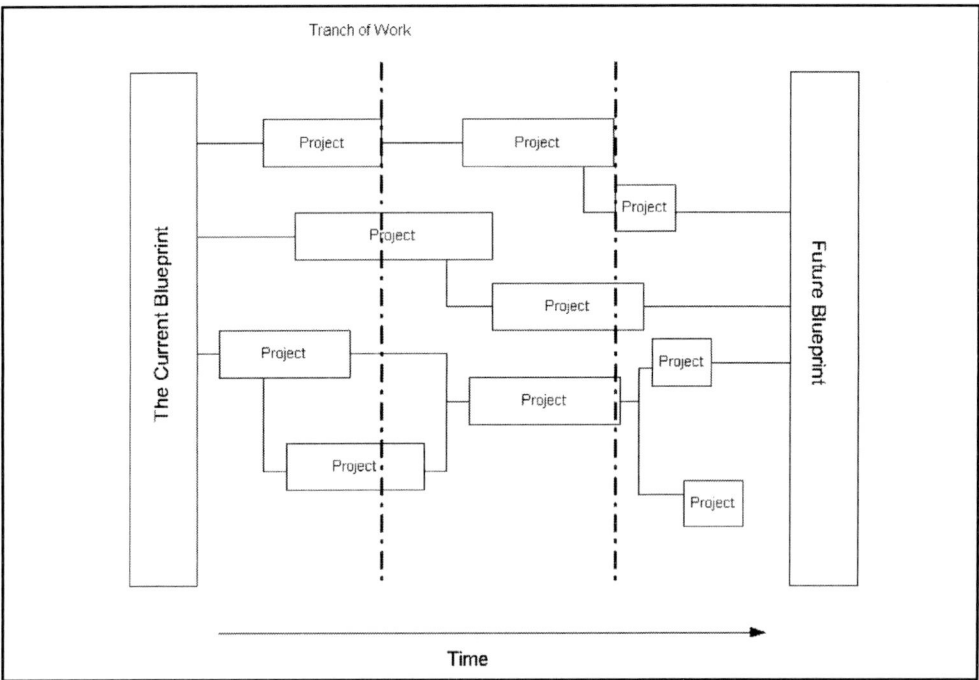

Multiple projects are run, some concurrently[1]. There is delivery of benefit as the programme progresses. Once the future blueprint is reached, the programme ends.

Employee utilisation

People are expensive, so it is important to make the best use of them.
Internal IT departments need to be able to determine their level of resource and the skills of each resource.

In planning for a financial year, it will be important to be able to distinguish what time is required to support existing systems and what is available for new developments. Effective planning is only possible if there is historical analysis available to see what was required in the past, and this can be mapped against a resource plan.

For professional services firms, the analysis of fee-earning time against total time available is paramount. Estimating the level of income will be difficult if time lost through non-conformance is not available. Without knowing what the number of

---

1 Adapted from *A Guide to Programme Management*, OGC

productive days is, together with time required to support sales effort, it will be difficult to accurately estimate what revenue can be earned.

To enable the calculation of actual employee utilisation, it is necessary to store a timesheet entry for every working day, that is, for the 253 working days in the year (the 'Resource planning' chapter explains how this figure is calculated).

Time will be logged not only on actual project work but also on projects where there is no deliverable but the employee is engaged in legitimate actions (such as holiday, training and so forth). The working year is divided into:

- working days
- non-productive days
- investment days
- revenue/productive days.

'Working days' are the total working days in a typical year (365 minus weekends and public holidays).
'Non-productive days' cover items such as holidays, sickness, and approved absence.
'Investment days' cover items such as training, pre-sales, technology reviews.
'Revenue/productive days' are the time then available to perform the actual work.

In setting up a system to record utilisation, there is a need for these 'dummy' projects to track non-productive and investment days.

Conclusion

The purpose of project and programme accounting is to ensure that costs and revenues are tracked and can be managed and improved upon. With a clear definition of 'What is a project?' and 'What is a programme?' not only can this tracking take place, but also like-for-like analysis can be performed.

Whether the programmes you run are in the runner, repeater, stranger model, or as a blueprint for change, there is still a need to report on the costs incurred and revenue received.

Consistent and comprehensive data structures will enable cross-project and programme reporting. This should lead to benefits from the focusing of management effort on key issues.

> *Hint:* If you are a newcomer to accounting, or are unsure of the way items are processed, it is worth investing in one of the PC accounting packages. The Quickbooks (www.quickbooks.co.uk) package has a navigator feature that shows the flow of information as a pictorial representation, a timesheet function and a payroll. For the cost of the package, it will show you in straightforward terms what happens.

BENEFITS

Benefits from introducing a project and programme accounting system can be split between financial and non-financial benefits. The financial benefits relate to those which increase revenue, reduce costs, improve profitability, and make better use of the resources available. The non-financial benefits relate to those which come from delivering a system, but do not necessarily relate directly to financial improvement.

Whether it is financial or non-financial benefit, this chapter uses the classifications for benefit analysis based on the Office of Government Commerce classes listed below.

Benefit classification

The OGC guide, *Managing Successful Programmes,* provides the following list of benefit classes. For the purposes of this chapter, Economy, Revenue Enhancement and Internal Management benefits are listed.

Benefit class	Description
Economy	Reducing costs whilst maintaining quality. This may be termed cost reduction.
Revenue enhancement and acceleration	Increasing revenue or bringing in the same revenue quicker, or both
Internal Management	Benefits which are internal to the organisation, such as improving the quality of decision-making or management productivity.
Policy or legal requirement (mandatory)	Benefits which allow an organisation to fulfil policy objectives or satisfy legal requirements, there the organisation has no choice but to comply.
Quality of Service	Benefits to customers, such as quicker response to queries, providing more detailed accurate information
Process Improvement (productivity or efficiency)	Benefits which allow an organisation to do the same job with less resource, allowing reduction in cost, or to do more.
Personnel or HR Management	The benefits of better motivated workforce may lead on to a number of other benefits – for example flexibility or increased productivity
Risk reduction	In business or technical terms this allows an organisation to be prepared for the future.
Strategic fit	Enabling the benefits of other systems to be realised.
Flexibility	Benefits that allow an organisation to respond to change without incurring additional expenditure

With acknowledgement to the Office of Government Commerce (OGC)

However, having a comprehensive project and programme accounting system should enable the realisation of benefits in process improvement, quality of service and risk reduction.

Economy

A comprehensive programme accounting and project accounting system makes it possible to identify the programme and project overruns by activity. The cost of this can be calculated. Management activity can then be focused on preventing this non-conformance occurring again.

What could this mean in financial terms? It might mean a reduction in the cost of running an IT team through more effective use of resources, or using this saving to increase the number of projects and programmes which are run each year.

	% improvement in efficiency		
Annual IT spend	1%	1.5%	2%
5,000,000	50,000	75,000	100,000
10,000,000	100,000	150,000	200,000
20,000,000	200,000	300,000	400,000

The simple table above shows the potential savings through small increases in efficiency. For example, if you are spending £10 million per annum on your IT team, a productivity increase of 1% is worth an additional £100,000 of IT budget.

Revenue enhancement

For organisations that are in the revenue-earning business, small improvements in efficiency can mean large improvements in profitability. Two more simple tables illustrate this in action.

Charged Days per Consultant	No of Consultants	Total days per annum	Average Charge Rate	Total Income
140	30	4,200	£850	£3,570,000
140	50	7,000	£850	£5,950,000
140	100	14,000	£850	£11,900,000

Total Income	% Net Profit	Net Profit
£3,570,000	8%	£285,600
£5,950,000	8%	£476,000
£11,900,000	8%	£952,000

So, if a consulting business is achieving:
- 140 charged days per consultant per annum
- an average charge rate per day of £850
- a net profit of 8% before tax

implementing a comprehensive project and programme accounting system which enables, following management action, an improvement in charged days by just 2%, gives:

Total days per annum	% improvement	Extra Charge Days			
4,200	2%	84			
7,000	2%	140			
14,000	2%	280			

Average Charge Rate	Extra Charge Days	Additional Income	Old Net Profit	New Net Profit	% Improvement
£850	84	£71,400	£285,600	£357,000	25%
£850	140	£119,000	£476,000	£595,000	25%
£850	280	£238,000	£952,000	£1,190,000	25%

Therefore, a 2% improvement in charged days gives a 25% improvement in net profit.

Internal management benefits

One of the challenges of management is to know where to focus activity. Should it be to:

a. reduce non-conformance
b. calculate what lines of business are profitable and focus on these
c. obtain efficiency savings therefore providing economy benefits
d. improve revenue streams through more effective resource allocation?

Where to start can be difficult to quantify.

The implementation of a comprehensive, well structured, project and programme accounting system will create a database of metrics that can be reported against.

Operational improvements

Consider if you can currently report on the questions in the table opposite. If not, then would the ability to do this enable you to initiate more effective management action?

Benefits

Analysis	Use of information
Operational	
Where is the time going by activity?	To understand the nature of the work performed and skills required.
What are the major groupings, if any, of projects, programmes, people, activities?	To look for common issues, and an appreciation of the business.
What is the average size of project (in days performed, in revenue, in cost)?	To look for common issues, and an appreciation of the business.
What is the average size of programme (in days performed, in revenue in cost)?	To look for common issues, and an appreciation of the business.
How long (from start date to completion date) is the average project or programme?	To enable better business planning, programme and project planning
What numbers of days are there between the date of the work and the date the timesheet was entered?	This is a key indicator of an employee's efficiency. It impacts on the reporting, invoicing and all subsequent functions.
What level of overtime was performed?	Significant amounts of overtime tire people. To perform their best, they need sleep and have a balanced lifestyle. Use this to understand the deficiencies from planning, forecasting and expectation management.
What was the overtime cost?	Supporting argument when trying to bring about changes in planning and forecasting techniques.
What level of expenses were incurred on the project or programme?	Should expenses be recovered from the customer?
How effective was the expense recovery?	Operational effectiveness of procedures for expense tracking and recovery.
Does the policy of expense recovery require changing based on geographical location of work?	If you know the geographical location of your sites (possible by the site address field in the Programme Accounting system), and the location of your offices, it is possible to calculate the distance between the two. By understanding this, you can see the impact on the Project team, as well as the expense implications.
What use was made of taxis?	In central London it is easy to jump into a taxi but could be more cost effective to use the underground or bus. Are employees able to change their habits to reduce costs?
How much use is made of hotels, air travel?	Booking hotels and flights takes significant time. On the next project or programme, negotiate into the contract that the customer arranges hotels, air travel etc. This will save the project or programme Office time and administrative overhead.
Are there any significant problems with a supplier?	Use the information to negotiate lower costs/better payment terms.

What is the number of days between the date the order was placed (from the customer) to:
  a. when the project or programme started (first timesheet date)
  b. when the first installation began
  c. when the invoice was first/last raised
  d. when the project or programme was completed?
	To calculate the manufacturing cycle time effectiveness[2].

2. The above table is an extract from the 'Reporting' chapter. Footnote 2 can be found on page 126.

Project and Programme Accounting

Services businesses

For those of you in the services business, consider if you can answer these points.

Analysis	Use of information
Operational Improvements	
What is the average/maximum/median number of days between the date of the work and the date the time was invoiced?	This is especially important for revenue planning, and understanding the operational efficiency of your business. (It will need to be analysed by contract type.)
What is the number of days from invoice date to cash received date?	This is important for cash-flow planning, contract style, operational processes.
On overruns, are there any areas that stand out (by project, by person, by activity, by customer, by product, by project manager)?	You can then focus your management effort on addressing these.
Which project manager produced the most/least revenue?	Reward the achievers; focus on the non-achievers.
Which consultant produced the most/least revenue?	Reward the achievers; focus on the non-achievers.
Which consultancy team produced the most/least revenue?	Reward the team leader; focus on the non-achiever.
Which consultant performed the most days (excluding non-productive time)?	If this is not the person who produced the most revenue, you need to understand why not.
What is the average revenue produced by a consultant (in a quarter, six months, year)?	Better business planning
What is the actual utilisation against budget (by person, by project, by programme)?	Understand the efficacy and efficiency of the team. Tells you how good your budgeting is. Also, what the link is to core competencies so you can see the relationship between skills and revenue.
If you are invoicing/costing by days, how many hours have been performed?	If the total hours/7.5 (or whatever your working hours in a day are) is materially more than the days charged, next time charge by the hour, not the day.
What is the level of cancellation time?	If there is a significant amount of cancellation time, charge a cancellation fee or look at how you negotiate the contract.
Does one customer/project or programme have a significant impact on the revenue stream?	One customer is too powerful. The programme when finishing will cause a lack of work.
On a project or programme, what is the % of revenue between time- and non-time-related items (for example consultancy revenue compared to the total of hardware, software, etc)?	Looking for patterns will assist in understanding the business. Likewise, with 'what if' analysis, it is possible to profile the effect of, eg, lowering software prices.

Strategic review

The purpose of the strategic review is to ensure that the business is moving in the right direction. Again, consider if you can report on some or all of the following.

Analysis	Use of information
Strategic review	
What is the split between projects and programmes supporting the existing infrastructure against new business initiatives?	To see if the company is improving its position or just standing still (probably going backwards.)
Which customer/internal department spent the most with you?	Find out and buy them lunch!
Which customer/internal department produced the least in profitable business?	Get them to go to your competitor!
What is the total revenue from change control notes raised?	Better understanding of additional revenue opportunities. If there is only cost, then model what areas are going wrong and feed back into the project or programme life cycle.
What is the total time from change control notes raised?	Better understanding of additional revenue opportunities. If there is only cost, then model what areas are going wrong and feed back into the project or programme life cycle. Furthermore, a significant number of change control notes could indicate that the project scope was not defined properly in the first place.
What activities, if any, are typically subcontracted out?	Decide if this is becoming a core competency. Subcontracting has its risks, as individuals can leave at short notice. Perhaps it is work which needs to be performed by a PAYE employee.
Are there indicators from the non-productive time analysis?	Examples to look for are excessive travelling time, computer failure, etc. Excessive travelling time to remote projects will not show as a project cost, just an overhead cost. Perhaps the time should be held against the project to get a truer reflection on total cost.
Which projects/programmes are most profitable as a % of turnover?	Is it worth selling more of these?
Which projects/programmes are least profitable as a % of turnover?	Is it worth dropping this as a service offering?
What is the total number of different programme offerings?	Do more programme services need to be developed, or perhaps some dropped?

Project and Programme Accounting

Analysis	Use of information
Strategic review (cont'd)	
What changes occurred in the budgets from inception to completion?	This is an important indicator to show the change in programme or project scope. Many changes in budget indicate a moving target, which is difficult to control.
What discounts off list price (should there be one) were offered to get the business?	This report will require some work. It will be necessary to compare the prices charged for capital items, non-capital items and consultancy against the published price list at the time. However, it is an important indicator to show whether the prices are being discounted heavily to get business, or is the current pricing policy correct?

A benefits model

Taking the benefits listed, and creating a list in Microsoft Excel, you get:

Benefit Counter	Description of Benefit	How delivered	Benefit Class	When Realised
B1	Focus management effort on reducing non-conformance	Reporting the types of activities which are not profitable / causing most problems	Internal Management	After 6 months (requires mngt input)
B2	Focus management effort on removing non-profitable business	Reporting the types of project / programme work which is not profitable	Internal Management	After 6 months (requires mngt input)
B3	Raise awareness on resources expended on new business initiatives	Through reporting time and resources expended on projects flagged as new business initiatives	Internal Management	After 6 months (requires mngt input)
B4	Raise awareness on resources expended on supporting the existing infrastructure	Through reporting time and resources expended on projects flagged as supporting existing infrastructure	Internal Management	After 6 months (requires mngt input)
B5	Reduce risks associated with having a lack of skills in the business	Ability to model skills of the individuals against the services which are offered	Internal Management	After 6 months (requires mngt input)
B6	Able to calculate the cost of projects which do not deliver	Through accurate reporting on resources expended against a project at activity level	Economy	After 6 months (requires mngt input)
B7	Reduce the cost of employing subcontractors	Through better analysis of spend by supplier and renegotiating terms	Economy	After 3 months (requires mngt input)
B8	Reduce the risk of employing subcontractors	Through the ability to report on the type of work (by activity) which they are doing and see if this relates to business critical projects	Risk Reduction	After 3 months (requires mngt input)
B9	Assist in effectively calculating the return on investment for a Programme or Project	Through strong programme and project cost reporting	Revenue enhancement and acceleration	After 1 year (requires mngt input)
B10	Reduce the risk of dependency on key people	By being able to report on the type of work people are doing and assess its importance to the business	Risk Reduction	After 6 months (requires mngt input)
B11	Focus management effort on developing profitable business	By being able to understand what business lines are profitable	Internal Management	After 6 months (requires mngt input)
B16	Assist in the productisation of projects which should reduce their cost to deliver	Through the implementation of a completeness of approach based on top down and bottom up planning which is linked to financial reporting	Revenue enhancement and acceleration	After 6 months (requires mngt input)
B17	Improved collection of sales invoices	By implementing a comprehensive system for ensuring that only collectable invoices are raised	Revenue enhancement and acceleration	After 3 months (requires mngt input)
B18	Improved cash management	By planning with an approach to automating cash flow forecasting based on agreed project plans	Revenue enhancement and acceleration	After 3 months (requires mngt input)
B19	Consistency of understanding of people costs	By agreeing a common cost per day based on an agreed cost with the Financial Director of the business	Economy	After 3 months (requires mngt input)
B20	Improved Expense Recovery	Through defining processes which capture expenses regularly which can then be recharged in a timely manner	Revenue enhancement and acceleration	After 3 months (requires mngt input)

Creating a pivot table of this data gives us:

Count of Count	When Realised			
Benefit Class	After 1 year (requires mngt input)	After 3 months (requires mngt input)	After 6 months (requires mngt input)	Grand Total
Economy		3	1	4
Internal Management		1	50	51
More motivated workforce			2	2
Revenue enhancement and acceleration	1	3	1	5
Risk Reduction		1	1	2
Grand Total	1	10	53	64

This shows that there are at least 64 benefits from implementing a comprehensive project and programme accounting system. The main bulk of these are internal management benefits.

DESIGN BASICS

Introduction

In implementing a system you need to design the data structures and understand the hierarchical relationships between activities, projects and programmes. Naturally there will be data which flows into and out of the system and this must be taken into consideration.

The basic design of a system includes:

a. *Process overview* This gives a model of data flows to show where information is to come from to 'feed' the accounting system.
b. *Relationships* This looks at the hierarchy of relationships from resource to activity, then up into project and programme.

For those of you who work with external organisations, customers and suppliers, then there is an added level of complexity.

The 'Advanced design concepts' chapter in Section Two then takes the relationship model further, defining hierarchies and nested programmes. These are extended to cover employees and skills.

Process overview

Every organisation has its own esoteric ways it works with its customers, suppliers, subcontractors and employees. This will require clarification (What systems are in place? What are the processing timescales?) before the process of improvement can take place.

First identify what are the component parts of the project or programme accounting system for your company. To do this, the information flow and relationships must be identified.

The types of questions to ask are:

Area	Questions
Materials	What material costs are incurred and are these recoverable/sold on? From where are they purchased? What are the terms of payment? Is there a distinction made at the moment on the reason for the purchase (for example, job analysis)? Who makes the purchase (for example, do external project personnel purchase materials on your behalf)?
People	Does the organisation use PAYE employees only? Does the organisation use subcontractors? What are the terms of engagement for a subcontractor? Is there a timesheet culture in place?

Area	Questions
Customers	What is the contractual relationship (for example, time and materials, fixed price, cost plus)? Do you have external customers (or are you an internal department servicing other departments)?
Overheads	How are overhead costs allocated (such as head office charges)?
Change control	Is there a process for tracking change control? Is it adhered to?
Reporting	Is there a process of reporting project and programme costs in place? Are the reports believed? Does a central repository, where project data is collected, exist at the moment?
Timesheets	Is there a time recording system in place? What level of granularity is recorded at the moment (for example, is it only by project or is it broken down into activities)?
Timeliness	For each of the above, what is the typical time between work being performed/items purchased and the information delivered for reporting analysis?
Cash	When is cash paid to your business? How is cash forecasted? When do you pay out to suppliers, subcontractors?

From this research, you should be able to baseline your position and work out what is required, either to improve existing systems or implement a new one.

Systems for project reporting

Let's assume that you are developing a new system for project and programme accounting. You will need a project repository, where all the costs, revenue, days, budgets and related financial and non-financial data can be stored.

At project start-up, the baseline information is entered. As the project progresses, the disparate sub-systems (purchasing, sales, time recording) are used to process transactions and feed the project repository.

The programme and project reporting is taken from the repository.

A typical information flow and project repository for an organisation that purchases

Design Basics

and sells on goods and services, as well as providing resources for its projects internally, would look like this:

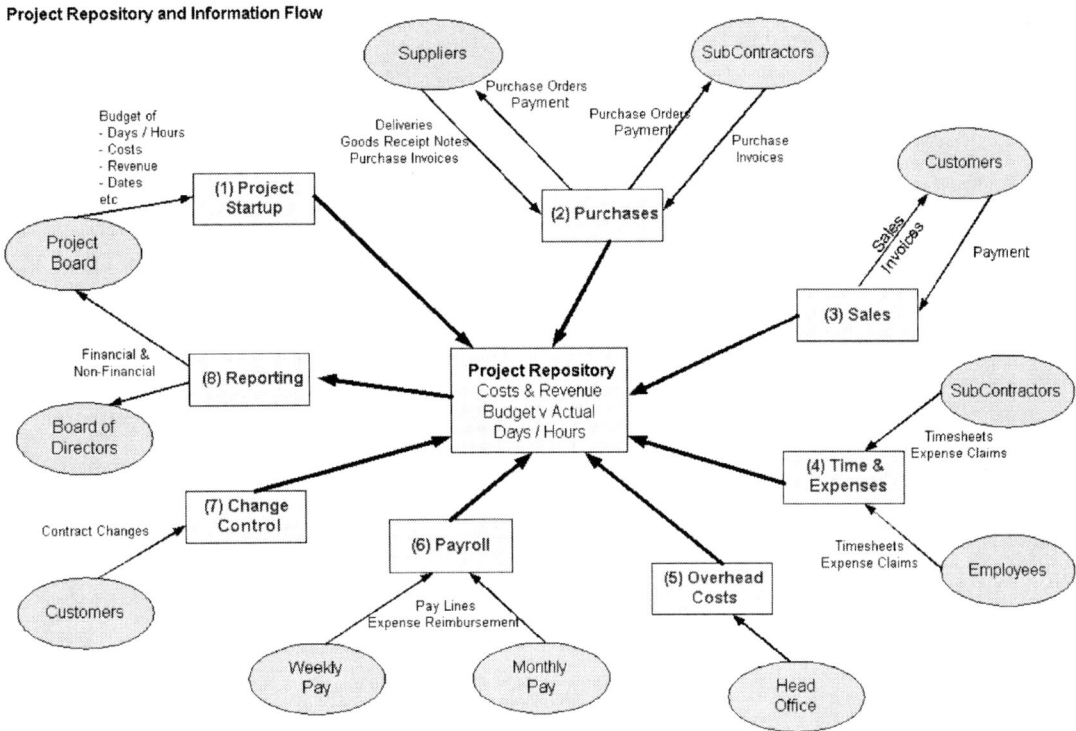

By understanding the individual elements, and what processes may already exist, the new or revised processes can be drawn up with a view to what is required to deliver them. The answers from your process analysis will enable the creation of an information flow map for your business.

(1) Project start-up
This collects data showing project name, start and end dates, project manager, activity, revenue and cost budgets, and other project initiation information. Typically this would come from the project board, the project sponsor or some other entity.

(2) Purchases
These are the goods and external services which are purchased for the project. In some organisations they may be bought and sold on, so there needs to be a link from the purchase to the sale. Typically the subcontractors are treated differently from buying items such as software.

(3) Sales
This is the revenue that is received for the project. The customer may well be another

part of the organisation. This sometimes happens in multinational companies where there is a consulting team who bid for work against external suppliers. The invoicing process is dealt with through cross-charging. In these instances cash might not change hands but there is tracking of revenue in the management accounts. (I once met a financial controller who called these 'wooden dollars'.)

(4) Time and expenses
This is the time expended by employees and subcontractors on the project. The expenses are out-of-pocket expenses which are incurred to deliver the project. Traditionally, timesheets used to be paper forms which were (sometimes!) returned in the post. Now electronic time-recording systems can be used, with timesheets entered weekly or monthly.

(5) Overhead costs
These are any overhead costs, such as floor-space charges, which are posted to the project or programme. The value and possible generation of these entries would come from an external entity, like head office. They are costs which are shown in the accounts, but are not likely to have any impact on the programme or project cash flow.

(6) Payroll
The time-recording system will show what time has been expended by each employee on what activities. However, this will not have the cost information, so it may be necessary to get payroll data. (Later I will look at the alternative of using standard costs per employee.)

(7) Change control
The function of change control in project and programme accounting is to ensure that changes are considered in the context of the business. For example, change control could realign delivery dates, but not increase the budgeted cost. You would need to be aware of this and evaluate the financial impact.

(8) Reporting
The reporting is to the project board, the programme board or board of directors of the business for the individual project. The level of reporting will depend on the demands of the business. Later I will consider the importance of being able to report across like-type projects and programmes.

Process with timing
Next, for each of the elements, you add the timing of the item; that is, when the information is normally submitted, or processing takes place.

In the example below, there is a combination of weekly, monthly and contractual terms. The items with contract terms indicate that these are subject to a contractual relationship. It is unlikely that there will be a linear timetable for spend and receipt of revenue.

Design Basics

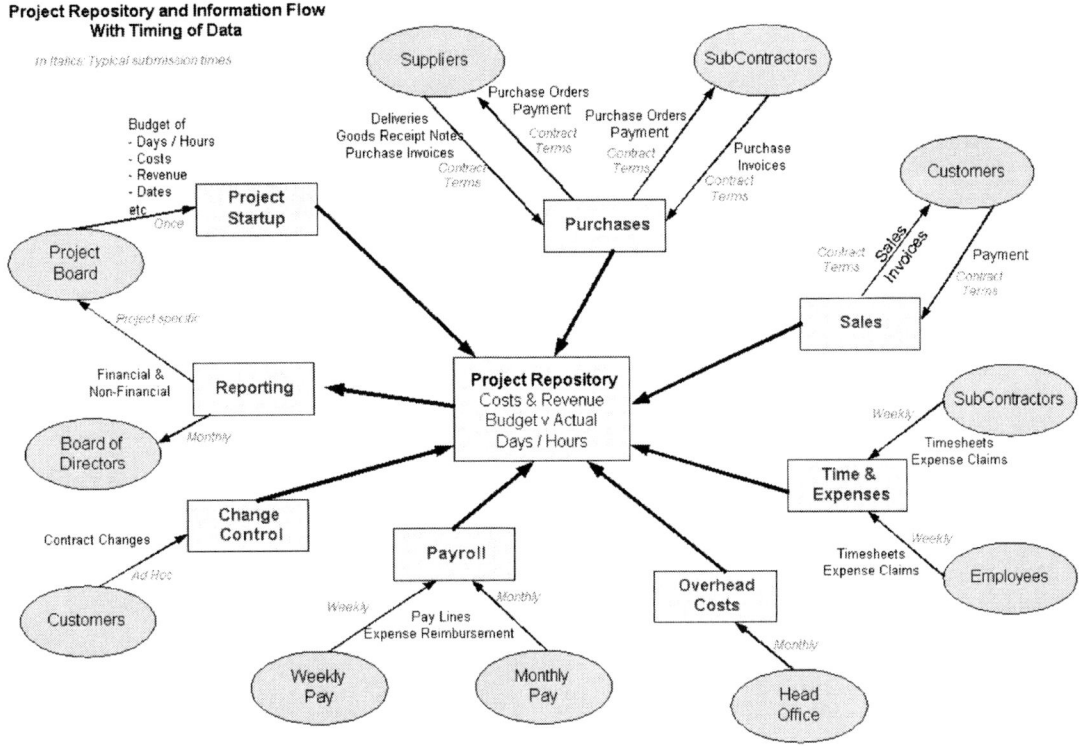

Project Repository and Information Flow With Timing of Data

When you add your timing I suggest that you expand it to include:

a. the project board
b. the suppliers and subcontractors
c. the customers
d. the employees
e. head office and how overhead costs are identified
f. what types of payroll are run
g. how change control is managed
h. the type of reporting and where that takes place.

Remember that if you work in a consulting business, the programme or project initiation comes from the initial sale. As senior supplier, if it is a PRINCE2-based project organisation, then you will be on the project board. It is unlikely that you will want to share cost information with your customer. They will be able to work out the expected gross profit and could use this in a negotiation against you in any revisions to contract which might be required.

Information flow optimised

Once you have a process flow, then you need to optimise the flow of data and bring in a commonality of data collection. This will assist in gathering data across all projects and

Project and Programme Accounting

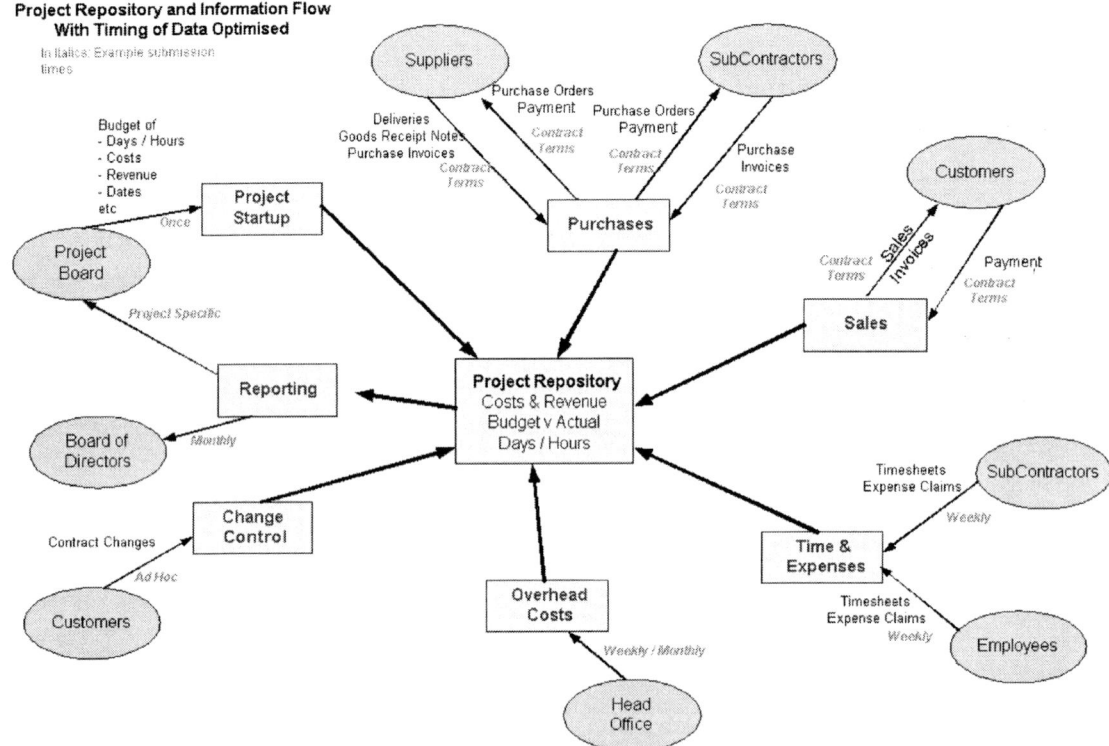

programmes. Also, the quicker the data capture, the better the project and programme control can be.

As you will see in the next chapter, 'Budgeting', there is a discussion on the calculation of payroll costs. My preference is to move to a standard employee cost and it is for this reason that the payroll box is dropped.

I prefer a standard cost as it avoids issues of payroll sensitivity, collects the numbers together in a timely manner, removes the need to worry about pay changes, and so on.

Relationships

Once you know the flow of information, and what is required (eg, weekly reporting) then it is necessary to define the relationships. By developing a schematic relationship of the hierarchy of activities through project to programme, the design of the comprehensive reporting solution is complete.

The entity relationship diagrams start from the simple customer–project relationship and can progress to the multiple programme, multiple customer, multiple project relationship. Entity relationship diagramming is a way of showing how items link together logically – not how they are actually stored on a hard disk. At this stage we are not so interested in the physical storage of data, but how the items relate to each other.

If you can picture the relationships in your mind, then, when implementing a system, it should be possible to conceptualise how the final system will be configured.

The entity relationship diagram

Entity relationship diagrams can be seen as building blocks in developing a logical view of the process links rather than the way in which the system will actually be implemented. From this view you can design an implementation which will meet not only the needs of one programme with multiple projects, but cross-programme and project reporting.

The approach used is based on entities where the notation for an entity (something you store information about) is a box. This is based on SSADM[1]. For example:

Basic entity   Programme   Project   Customer

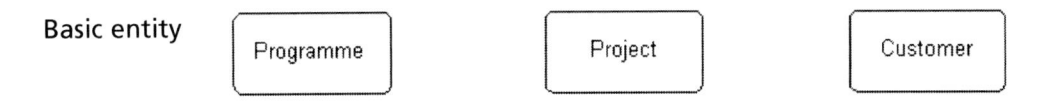

How do you relate entities?

Entities are related using a line. The example below shows that a programme contains one project and that project belongs to the programme in a one-to-one relationship:

One-to-one

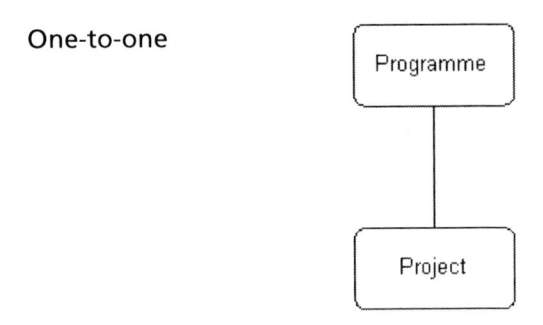

Of course, nothing is ever this simple; so, in the next example, a programme contains one or more projects. Each project belongs to a programme:

One to many relationship

Crows foot used to represent one-to-many relationships

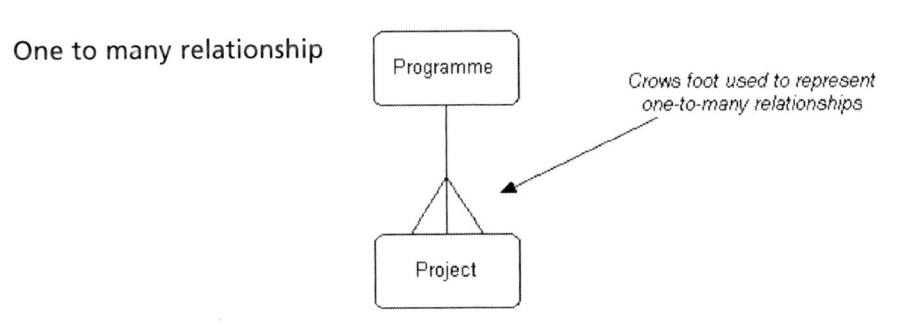

There are circumstances where the relationship is optional:

---

1. *Data modelling, business systems development with SSADM*, OGC, ISBN 011330871-X

Optionality of relationships

```
        ┌─────────┐
        │ Project │
        └────┬────┘
             ╎         The Master Entity can exist
             ╎         without the detail - detail cannot
             ╎         exist without the master
             ╎
           ╱─┴─╲
          ╱──┬──╲
        ┌─────────┐
        │ Activity│
        └─────────┘
```

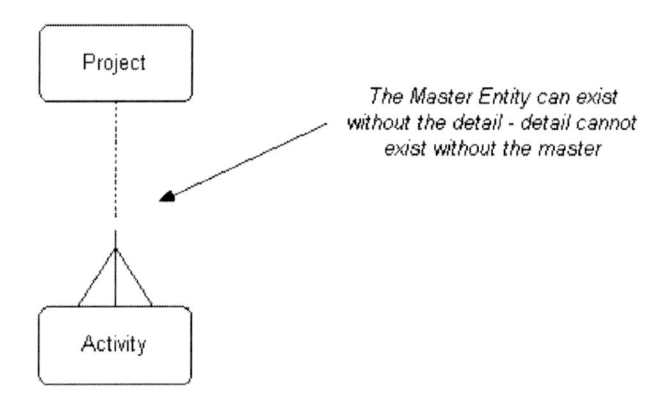

A project may have one or more activities. An activity cannot exist without a project. Note that all entities are shown in the singular.

It is this notation which will be used to demonstrate pictorially the relationships which need to be considered when designing a solution.

A final consideration is the use of relationship labels. Each label describes the relationship from the point of view of the entity to which it is nearest:

Optionality of relationships

```
        ┌─────────┐
        │ Project │
        └────┬────┘
             ╎ Consists of
             ╎
             ╎
  to deliver a╱─┴─╲
            ╱──┬──╲
        ┌─────────┐
        │ Activity│
        └─────────┘
```

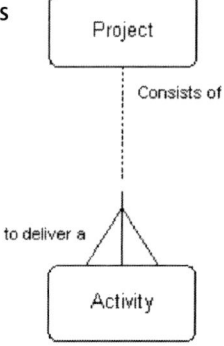

So here you see that a project consists of one or more activities. Each activity is there to deliver a project.

Simple relationship examples

The simple relationships which are defined below include:

- One customer has one or more projects but no programme
- One programme has one or more projects
- One customer has one or more programmes
- One programme has one or more customers.

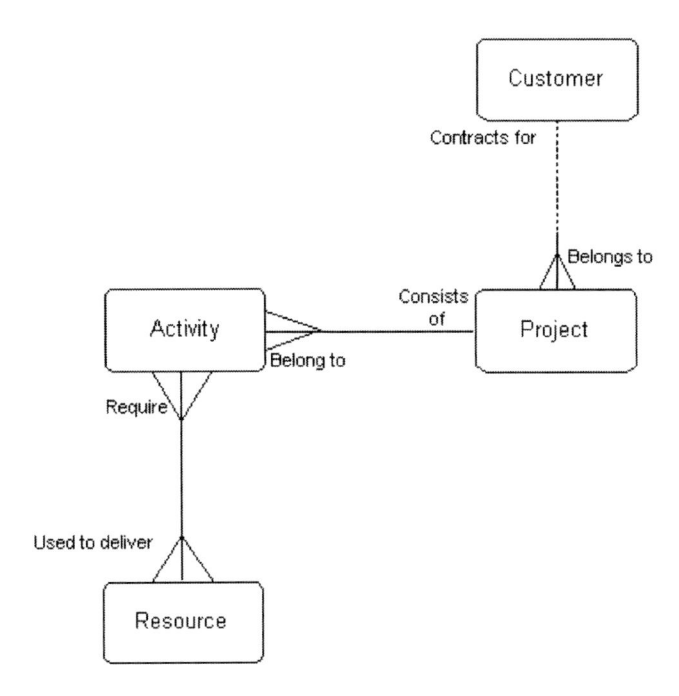

One customer has one or more projects but no programme

```
                              ┌──────────┐
                              │ Customer │
                              └──────────┘
                          Contracts for  │
                                         │
                                         │
                                         ▲ Belongs to
                           Consists   ┌─────────┐
         ┌──────────┐         of      │ Project │
         │ Activity │◄──────────────► └─────────┘
         └──────────┘  Belong to
              │
         Require
              │
         Used to deliver
              │
         ┌──────────┐
         │ Resource │
         └──────────┘
```

Here is a customer who has one or more projects. Each project has one or more activities. Each activity uses one or more resources. Resources, in this instance, are people, hardware, software, capital items and so forth. Each resource can be used on multiple activities. The activity belongs to a project.

For those of you who consider that there cannot be a many-to-many relationship, I will leave it to you to model the structure further. It is the meaning of the relationship that is important at this stage.

Question: Can you identify and report this from your system? Could you identify the different types of projects which take place in your organisation? Is the activity analysis consistent across like project types?

Project and Programme Accounting

One programme has one or more projects

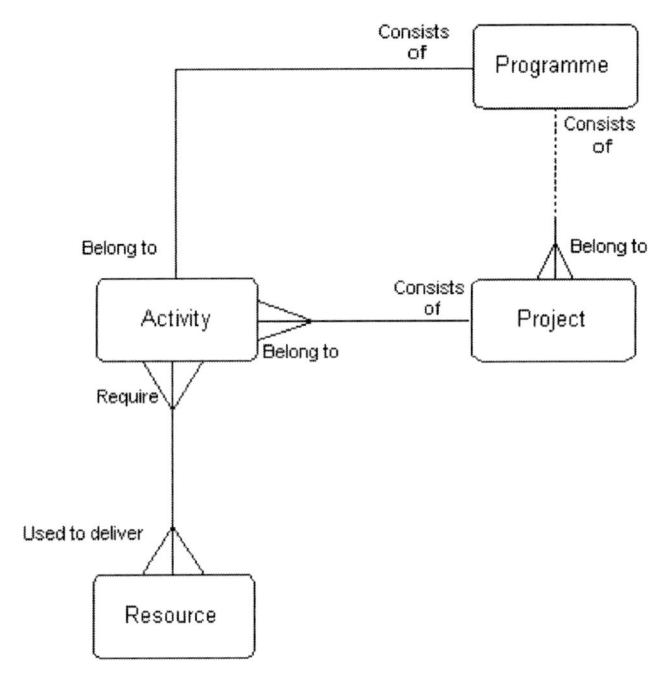

The above shows where a programme contains one or more projects. The link from programme to activity is to indicate that there are activities which are performed by the programme: for example, the programme meetings, the writing of the programme brief and so forth.

You may consider that the programme itself has a project that is the running of the programme – the internal mechanism. I have chosen not to use this approach.

Question: Can you identify and report this from your system?

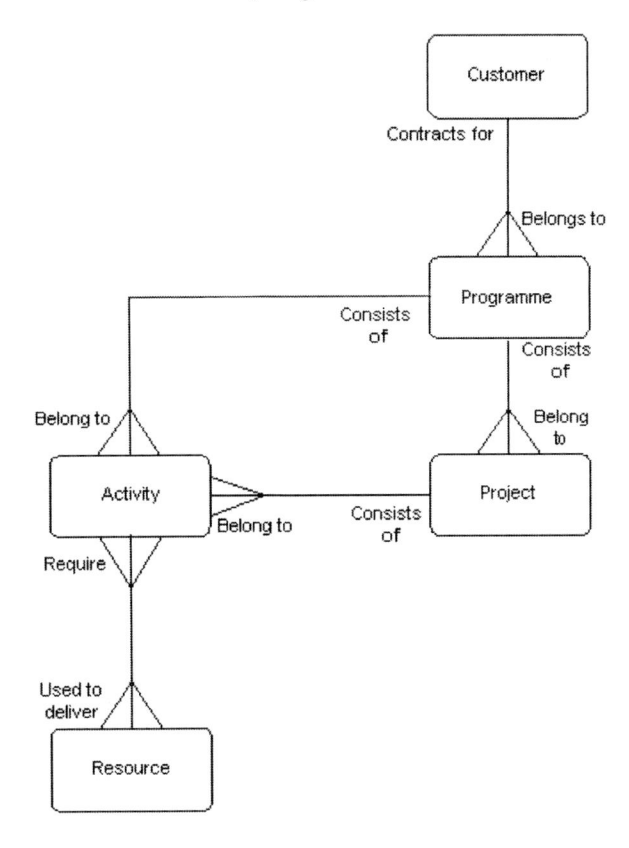

One customer has one or more programmes

```
                          Customer
                             |
                      Contracts for
                             |
                        Belongs to
                             △
                         Programme
              Consists   ┌────┐
                of       │    │ Consists
                         │    │   of
         Belong to       │    │  Belong
              △          │    │    to
          Activity       │    │  Project
              │ Belong to│    │
              │          Consists
         Require         of
              △
           Used to
           deliver
              △
          Resource
```

Here a customer has one or more programmes under way. The programme belongs to the customer. As in the previous diagram, the activity is linked both to the programme and the project.

A company which charges for programme management will have customers (in the debtor sense). An IT department could consider that the other departments it works with are its customers; albeit they are internal customers. Other departments are then considered in the same was as an external customer and afforded the same level of service. Furthermore, the cost (to a department) of a system can be modelled in the same way it would be if it were sourced from an external supplier.

Question: Can you identify and report this from your system? Do you group like projects together under a programme as a way of managing multiple projects (remembering the example of Runners, Repeaters and Strangers)?

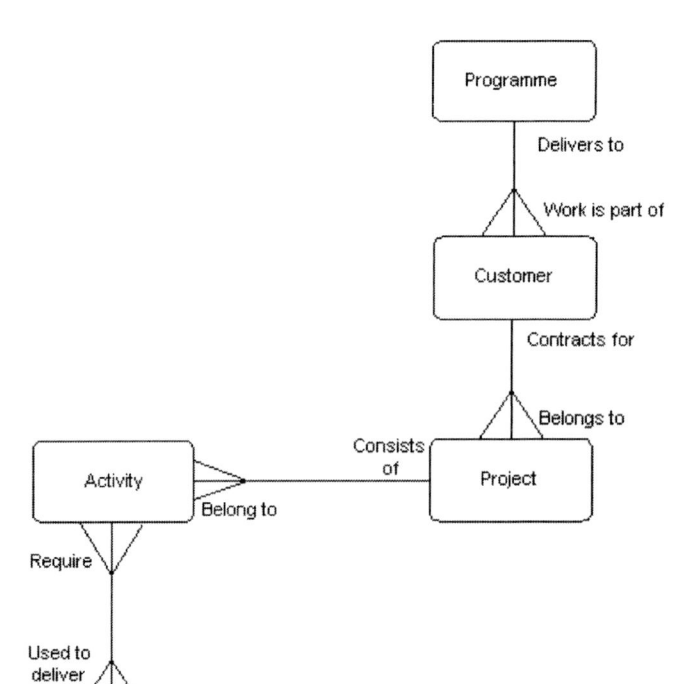

One programme has one or more customers

You will recall that some organisations use programme management as a way of running their business. In this case the organisation will have multiple customers, each of whom have one or more projects under way.

For example, a company that implements and supports financial accounting systems will perform a number of upgrades to the latest release of their accounting system, for their customers. The upgrade projects are of a 'like type' so can be considered 'runners'. A programme is run each financial year to support the upgrade 'runner' projects. The projects are for discrete customers. A customer may elect to upgrade more than once during the year (depending on the release schedule of the new software).

Conceptualising in this way, you can identify the successful and non-successful activities. For instance, during a software upgrade, if there are consistent problems, these can be identified. The repository of activity data will enable meaningful analysis.

Question: Can you identify and report this from your system?

A programme is an organisation

So far, the design process has considered the situation with one or more programmes running, each of which contains a number of projects. But the programme may be the organisation.

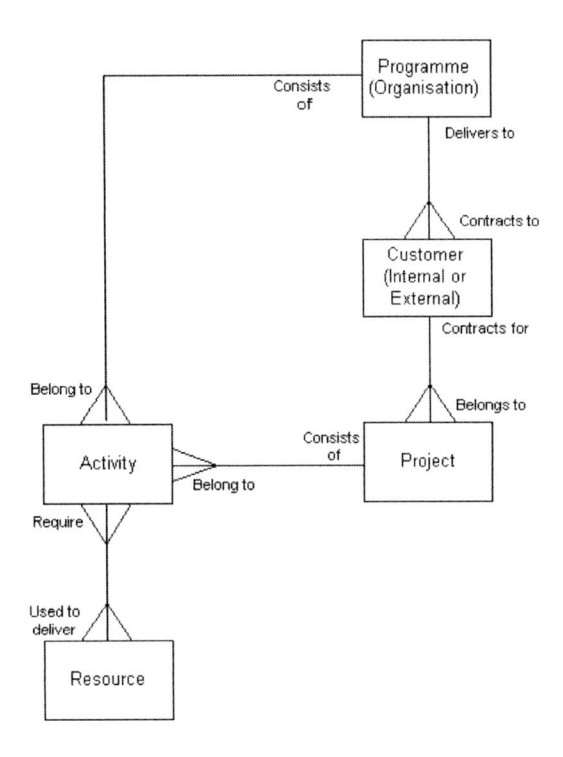

Such an organisation will run multiple projects each year, with projects run as part of the work of the organisation. The customers could be external organisations, or internal departments regarded as customers.

This data modelling can assist in understanding the alignment of company strategy and operation to programme, then to project, and so to the performance of individual resources.

Conclusion

The purpose of this chapter is to get you thinking how you could implement a project or programme accounting system.

The first stage is to define how data is to be collected, ie, the process flows showing where data is coming from and information going to. Secondly, to consider how the items are to be analysed hierarchically, and whether programme management is to be used as a management tool for running multiple projects.

BUDGETS

Introduction

Typically, companies budget by department and cost centre based on a hierarchical structure. The problem is that projects and programmes will cut across these traditional structures.

Let's have a look at the differences and then I'll explain how budgets are broken down for projects and programmes, and the relationship to financial accounting.

You may be wondering why this was not covered in the Design Basics chapter. Well, budgets are an intrinsic part of the project or programme/activity/resource. So I have not split them out on the entity relationship diagram. For clarity the relationships are detailed below.

Company versus project and programmes

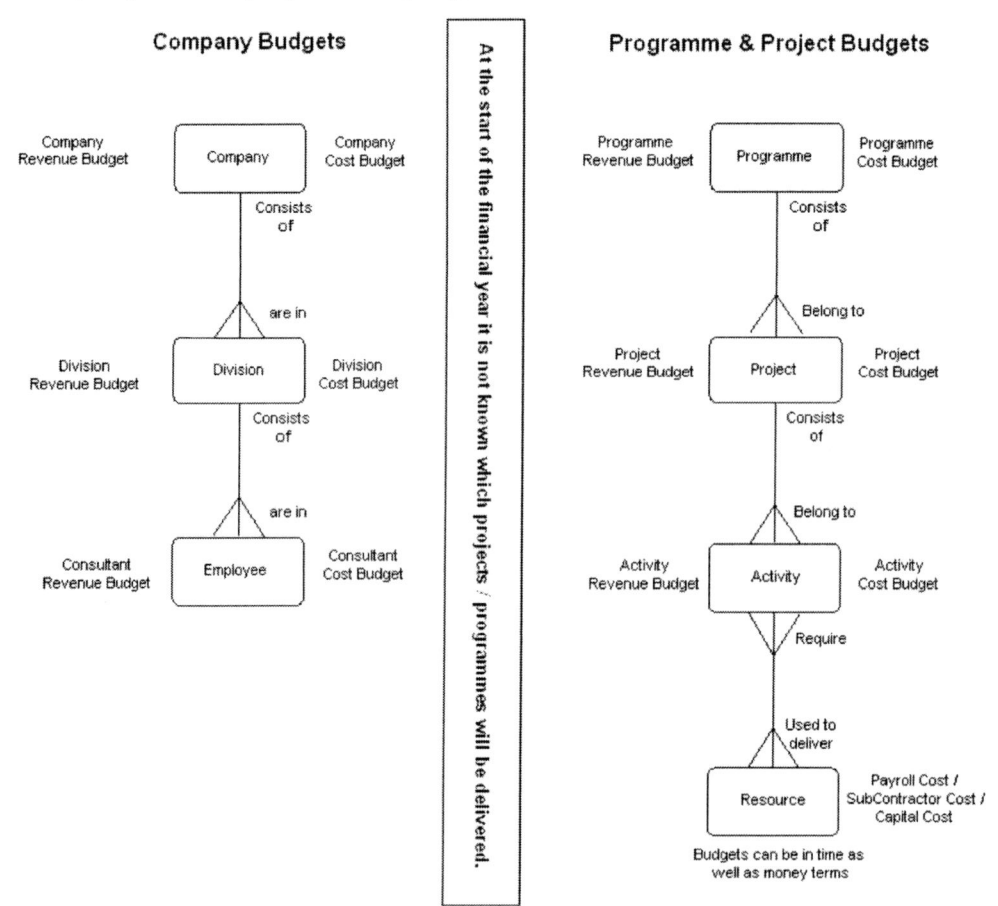

Company Budgets

- Company Revenue Budget — Company — Company Cost Budget
  - Consists of
- Division Revenue Budget — Division — Division Cost Budget
  - are in
  - Consists of
- Consultant Revenue Budget — Employee — Consultant Cost Budget
  - are in

At the start of the financial year it is not known which projects / programmes will be delivered.

Programme & Project Budgets

- Programme Revenue Budget — Programme — Programme Cost Budget
  - Consists of
- Project Revenue Budget — Project — Project Cost Budget
  - Belong to
  - Consists of
- Activity Revenue Budget — Activity — Activity Cost Budget
  - Belong to
  - Require
- Resource — Payroll Cost / SubContractor Cost / Capital Cost
  - Used to deliver

Budgets can be in time as well as money terms

If you consider the company budget on the left, which will be a cost and revenue budget, can this be reconciled against the programme and project budget on the right? Depending on the type of organisation, the reconciliation could be for a subset only of a company budget. For many organisations, it is unlikely that the number, type and scope of projects and programmes are known at the start of the year. Note that project and programme revenue budgets might only be for organisations who charge for their services.

Resources clarification

The resource entity can be clarified further. For example, in a project, the relationship between activity and resource requires a combination of people and materials.

The materials may be both capital and non-capital together with an element of miscellaneous items. In accounting terms this is an important distinction. The capital items can be depreciated over a number of years, while the non-capital items are shown as costs in the profit and loss account for that period. There is an explanation of this later in the chapter.

Breaking the resource section down, we get:

Programme & Project Budgets

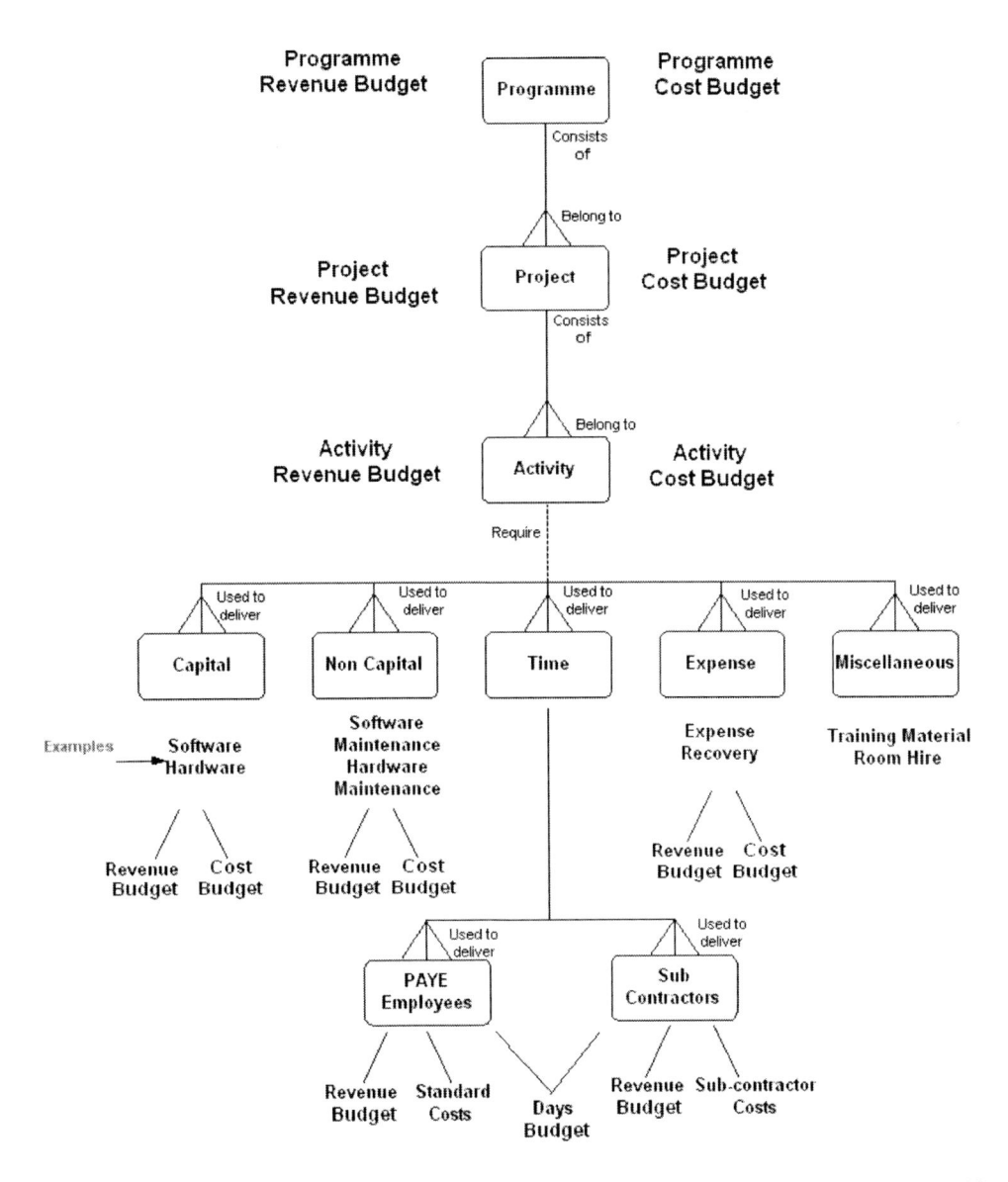

```
                    Programme                            Programme
                  Revenue Budget      [Programme]       Cost Budget
                                          |
                                     Consists of
                                          |
                                      Belong to
                                          |
                     Project                              Project
                  Revenue Budget       [Project]        Cost Budget
                                          |
                                     Consists of
                                          |
                                      Belong to
                                          |
                     Activity                             Activity
                  Revenue Budget       [Activity]       Cost Budget
                                          |
                                       Require
       ┌──────────────┬──────────────┬──────────────┬──────────────┐
    Used to        Used to        Used to        Used to        Used to
    deliver        deliver        deliver        deliver        deliver
   [Capital]    [Non Capital]     [Time]        [Expense]    [Miscellaneous]

                    Software                       Expense       Training Material
  Examples → Software  Maintenance                 Recovery        Room Hire
             Hardware  Hardware
                       Maintenance
          /      \      /      \                  /      \
     Revenue   Cost   Revenue  Cost            Revenue   Cost
     Budget   Budget  Budget  Budget           Budget   Budget

                             Used to            Used to
                             deliver            deliver
                              [PAYE]              [Sub
                            Employees          Contractors]
                           /      \            /         \
                      Revenue  Standard   Revenue    Sub-contractor
                      Budget    Costs     Budget        Costs
                                  Days
                                 Budget
```

29

The revenue budget is applicable where the organisation charges for its services, resells the capital items, and so forth.

Budgeting for cost and revenue

To explain the diagram, let's look at the implementation of a comprehensive, integrated, IT system consisting of a number of component projects.

The main cost areas would be:

Area	Example
Capital items	Software
	Hardware
	Communication and WAN infrastructure
Non-capital Items	Software maintenance
	Hardware maintenance
Time	PAYE employees
	Subcontractors (there are instances where subcontract costs can be posted as capital expenditure items, so it would be worth checking with your finance department)
Expenses	Reimbursed expenses
Miscellaneous	Training rooms
	Equipment hire (eg, overhead projects, lite-pro's, etc.)

Capital items

At the start of the budgeting process, the particular modules required for the system implementation will be identified. There is a capital cost for the organisation in buying these.

Software and hardware are used against multiple activities. For example, the configuration of a system cannot take place without the software. Likewise, the end-user training will need software.

The distinction is important, as a capital item will be depreciated over a number of years. For example: a computer is bought for £3,000 and depreciated over 3 years based on a straight-line depreciation of one third per annum. So, the costs which go into the profit and loss account are £1,000 per annum, not the total £3,000.

The capital items will appear on the asset register. This means that they have value to the organisation. It is possible, in some instances, to capitalise the time spent on a project or programme and depreciate that cost over a period. For example, if you are writing a piece of software which is then used over a number of years, the time spent to design, write, test and implement the system is a people cost. However, the output from this is software which can be used by the organisation in the furtherance of its objectives.

UK Government and resource accounting and budgeting

If you are working in the public sector in the UK, accounting used to be based on what is known as cash accounting. In the 2002 Spending Review, there was the full implementation of resource budgeting. HM Treasury Paper 'Better Management of Public Services November 2001' said that resource accounting and budgeting '…delivers a step change in the management of capital – both in the utilisation of existing assets and new investment'.

I recommend checking with your finance department over the capitalisation policy. For each project and programme, list the outputs, the cost of delivering those outputs and then, with your finance director, identify which can be capitalised, put on the asset register and understand how they are treated subsequently in the accounts.

Try and get an understanding of this early on in the programme. It is more efficient (and less troublesome) to collect the data correctly in the first instance rather than try and backwardly calculate the figures after the event!

Non-capital items

A non-capital item will be a cost which is incurred and written off in the current profit and loss account. It is not depreciated over a number of years. An example of this is software maintenance.

Time

Time has its own esoteric issues. Financial budgeting is performed in money terms. Yet estimating is in days and hours, so you need a mechanism to convert time to money.

By breaking down the work into distinct activities, identifying an estimate for each activity and the resources needed, it is possible to calculate the total work. For instance:

work = duration x resources (in Microsoft Project)

With a days or hours estimate this needs to be translated into a cost (£). At first sight, this appears to be easy. Take the annual salary for each person, divide by the number of working days and then by the working hours in a day.

For example:

Annual salary	£40,000
Daily amount	£40,000/252 working days
	£158 per day
Hourly amount	£158/8 hours per day
	£19.75 per hour

Project and Programme Accounting

With a daily amount, you do not have to worry about full-time or part-time employees. Simply multiply their number of hours by the hourly amount and that will give you the person's cost. If only it were that simple!

The cost of employing a person is more than just their salary. Likewise the number of working days does not equate to the number of productive days.

There are 11 distinct areas we need to understand for budgeting purposes:

1. Calculating the number of days required to deliver the programme or project
2. The relationships between items
3. Sensitivity of data
4. Timeliness
5. Calculating the annual package
6. Obtaining the data and calculating values
7. Using a standard cost
8. Subcontractors
9. Revenue recognition
10. Reporting actual against budget
11. Reconciliation.

PRINCE2

For the PRINCE2 purist, the starting point is the deliverable/product. What product is being produced and then what activities are required to complete that product? This is an additional relationship to consider.

Calculating the number of days required

There are a number of ways to calculate the expected number of days required to deliver a project. For example, in software development the early methods relied on estimating the number of lines of code. By understanding how many lines could be written by a person in a day, it was believed that it was possible to calculate the total time to complete a program.

However you attempt to do it, you need to identify an estimate (preferably accurate) of the time to perform activities. These are then rolled up into the project or programme to give a total time. From this, the expected cost (in people terms) can be calculated.

The details given below are based on a bottom-up approach to calculating the days required. The important point is to ensure that the estimate can be aligned with the actual to allow for analysis of overrun/under-run by activity or group of activities.

Activity analysis

In the entity relationship chart, I divided the project and programme into activities. The activities will be in the estimation model, tracked to the project or programme plan, and then with time recorded against them.

So, a start point could be bottom-up estimating, where for each project in the programme:

- all the activities are identified
- for each activity,
   - the expected duration is assigned
   - the expected resources required are assigned
- the projects are combined together to give a total duration of time which can be modelled by:
   - project
   - person
   - activity
   - programme (where there are multiple projects).

The project view

When defining activities, the key is to ensure consistency throughout (from the activity planning through to the budgeting, the time recording and subsequent cross-project correlation). For example, when implementing a system, your project will commence with project initiation.

If you budget* as follows:

Phase	Activities	Time
Project initiation	Initiation meeting	1 day
	Write project initiation document	2 days
	Prepare first cut project plan	1 day
	Present project initiation document & project plan	0.5 days
	Provision for rework	0.5 days
	Total time	5 days

on your activity plan you have

Project initiation   5 days

and in the activity schedule for time recording:

Phase	Activities	Time
Project initiation	Initiation meetings	1.5 days
	Write project initiation document & project plan	3 days
	Provision for rework	0.5 days
	Total time	5 days

Both show that project initiation takes five days but they are clearly inconsistent in detail.

---

* OK, so your project initiation is likely to take longer than five days, but the point I am making is about consistency of data. This will become apparent as you read on.

Furthermore, your team will be confused and it will not be possible to track back over- or under-runs to any particular activity, only a group of activities.

The grouping, such as project initiation, might be at too high a level to enable management to initiate actions to remove any non-conformance in a focused way.

So, I would strongly recommend that the budget through to plan through to activities on timesheets is consistent (recognising different levels of granularity). Furthermore, with a realistic level of detail you can get a good grasp of the project or programme thus:

Project budget

Phase	Activities	Time
Project Initiation	Initiation meeting	1 day
	Write project initiation document	2 days
	Prepare first-cut project plan	1 day
	Present project initiation document & project plan	0.5 days
	Provision for rework	0.5 days
	Total time	5 days

Project plan

Name	Start date	Finish date	Duration
Project initiation	Wed 19/07	Tue 25/07	5 days
Initiation meeting	Wed 19/07	Wed 19/07	1 day
Write project initiation document	Thu 20/07	Fri 21/07	2 days
Prepare first-cut project plan	Mon 24/07	Mon 24/07	1 day
Present project initiation document & project plan	Tue 25/07	Tue 25/07	0.5 days
Provision for rework	Tue 25/07	Tue 25/07	0.5 days

Timesheet entry

You need to decide on the level of detail required from users when entering timesheets.

My experience is that in project status reporting, totalling up to major phases achieves clarity and brevity. Being able to identify the time at a lower level will ensure that detailed analysis is possible.

The relationships between items
The relationship between items represents the physical design of the system.

Programme to Project Activity

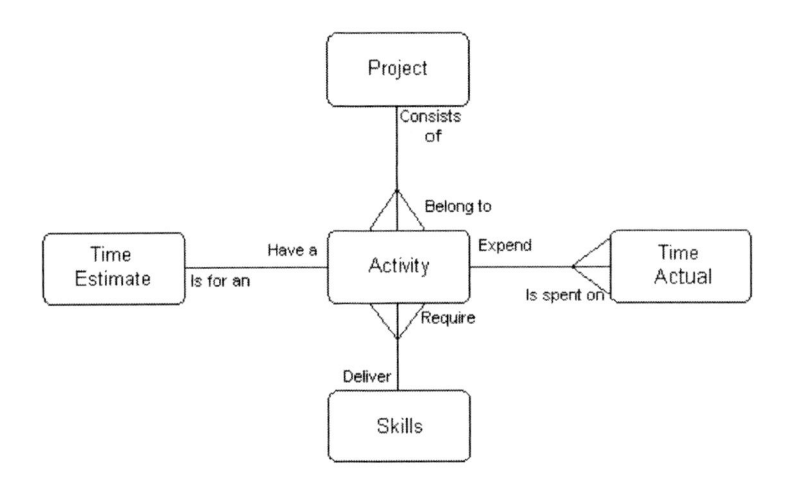

```
                    Project
                       |
                   Consists
                      of
                       |
                   Belong to
         Have a        |        Expend
Time  ---------- Activity ---------- Time
Estimate  Is for an    |   Is spent on  Actual
                    Require
                       |
                    Deliver
                       |
                     Skills
```

1. The project has a number of activities.
2. Each individual activity may have a time estimate (although I have shown this as a mandatory link).
3. The actual time expended is shown as a one-to-many relationship. The reason is best explained with an example:
   - Consider you are installing software
   - You have four days' work to be done
   - This is scheduled for 1 person for 3 days and a separate person for 2 x 0.5 days
   - In the time-recording system, this will be entered in as at least 5 different entries, being 3 for the first person at 1 per day and 2 for the second person at 1 entry for each of the 0.5 days.
4. The activity will require skills to deliver the activity. If the person you are using is not very well skilled then the time required is likely to be longer than if you had used a more experienced individual.

   In starting to identify the activities, you will soon find that an enormous list is created which at first sight appears unmanageable. It would be difficult to answer the question 'What level of detail is correct for your circumstances?' in the pages of a book. However, I offer the following guidance.

1. Identify the types of service you provide. For example:
   a. Software installation
   b. Software upgrades
   c. New feature training
   d. User training
   e. Implementation of a software module.

2. Break a sample of these down into component parts. Taking 'a' and 'b' above as the worked examples, the activities are:

Installation	Upgrade
• order software • deliver to site • install software on server • install software on workstations • restore demonstration database • test software • set up printers • demonstrate to users • sign off installation	• order software • deliver to site • install software on server • install software on workstations • restore demonstration and live databases • test software • set up printers • demonstrate to users • sign off installation

The difference is in the restoration of data. On an upgrade you need to restore the live transactions files as well.

3. Consider if the itemising of each item will add value to your understanding of the process. My own approach is (where possible) to quote, plan, budget and record actual data at a header level, eg, Installation or Upgrade but break out items which are clearly separate, such as testing an installation from a remote site. Additional breakdown is sometimes required on the project plan. The important point is consistency so the data can be reviewed.
4. Consider if the itemising of each item will be correctly recorded in the time-recording system. Eg, can you budget the time to install software on a server as opposed to a workstation? If you can, would it be accurately entered into the time-recording system by the person doing the work?
5. Consider if it is possible to give accurate guidance on the individual activities. Eg, pre-defined test scripts could give an indication of how long the 'test software' will take. Without predefined scripts, you could find yourself pulling numbers from the air.
6. Does the analysis add value to your business? For example, your project manager may spend time with the credit controller ensuring invoices are being paid by the customer. It is unlikely that you can charge for this time, but nevertheless if your cash is being collected then your business will be healthier. Do you create this as an activity on the project or programme or as a separate project that is chasing cash? It is the understanding of the issue that is important. The level of granularity which might, in the design context, seem to be perfect, could be too detailed, making the solution unworkable.
7. Is it possible to train the person to perform a group of activities or an individual activity? In the use of team performance codes, we are trying to understand an individual's efficacy.

Remember, the purpose is to create a set of activities, which can be:
1. used at the project level
2. rolled up for cross-project analysis at the programme level.

If you are a PRINCE purist, in defining your approach to activity analysis, you could start with the deliverable. The deliverable might be installed software, the activities:
- order software
- deliver to site
- install software on server
- install software on workstations
- restore demonstration database
- test software
- set up printers
- demonstrate to users
- sign off installation.

Privacy of data

In many organisations, payroll data is sensitive. Employee salaries and benefits are not published. It is up to individuals to tell their peers what they earn. Companies rarely put up a list of salary packages on the notice board; but larger organisations often have pay scales and band job roles within them.

The obstacle to calculating the employee cost is that, in a project or programme, it is unlikely you will be told the total salary package the person receives. Below is an approach to calculating standard employee costs which overcomes this issue.

Timeliness

A significant challenge is timeliness. When reporting programme or project progress against the actual time expended, this needs to be done quickly, ie, the time should not represent something which took place months ago.

By waiting until month end before knowing the costs, or year end for profit-related pay, the age of the data will mean its applicability will be lost or is of less value.

Calculating the annual package

The employee salary package is typically made up of a number of items. The days of a basic salary and that's your lot have gone. On a payslip there may be a number of lines such as:

Basic salary
London weighting
Car allowance
Bonus
Profit-related pay

Additional benefits provided may include:

Pension
Personal petrol
Fully expensed mobile phone
Car (in place of car allowance)
Car insurance
Car servicing
Medical insurance.

Project and Programme Accounting

These latter items are not likely to be stored in the payroll system or, if they are, an individual's details are unlikely to be released. A further consideration is that the company car could be owned or lease hired.

There are overhead costs which must also be taken into account:
- Office space
- Office furniture
- Heating
- Lighting
- Telephone
- Fax
- Computer
- Printer
- Paper.

The UK Government, of course, will ask the company to pay National Insurance contributions as well as the employees. These contributions are around 10% of the salary and there is no upper earnings limit on the company payments.

While the first problem is the privacy of the data, the second is that the cost of employing a person is more than their basic salary or salary package. There are overhead costs as well as items such as car servicing and insurance which might need to be taken into account.

Obtaining the data and calculating values

Here is an example of building a cost profile for an employee on a £40,000 salary.

Description	Where stored	Value per annum	Comment	App'x
Basic salary	Payroll	£40,000		No
London Weighting	-	-	Not applicable	-
Car allowance	-	-	None: receives a car	-
Car	Purchase ledger	£4,800	Leased at £400 per month	No
Car servicing	Expenses	£200	Employee claims back servicing cost	Yes
Car insurance	Purchase ledger	£600	Group-wide policy which works out at £600 per employee	Yes
Bonus	Payroll	£3,200	Performance bonus, maximum amount based on a quarterly bonus of £800	Yes
Profit-related pay	Payroll	£6,000	Approximate annual PRP bonus equivalent to 15% of basic salary	Yes
Pension	Nominal ledger	£2,000	Paid direct to a company scheme at 5% of basic salary	No
Personal petrol	Expenses	£1,200	Worth around £100 per month	Yes
Mobile phone	Purchase ledger	£100	Includes line rental and cost of call. Approximate figure	Yes
Computer	Fixed assets	£1,000	Taken as £3,000 (computer, software, etc) depreciated over 3 years	Yes
Telephone	Purchase ledger	£50	Approximate amount for calls made when in the office	Yes
	Total	£59,150		

Taking the basic salary of the employee and adding in benefits and overheads has given a figure 50% more than the starting point! Furthermore, this does not include office space, expenses incurred at work and other costs.

If we want to reconcile the figures against the financial accounts, it will be necessary to split them out as they are entered.

For example: pension payments are likely to be one amount, with a sheet sent to the pension provider detailing how the money is to be allocated. To get a breakdown for the project, it would be necessary to give line item transactions a project reference. If someone worked on more than one project, then the time split would be required so the correct allocation can take place. This is additional work for the accounts department. As the data is confidential, it is not likely that they would tell you anyway!

Furthermore, nine of the entries are approximate. At the start of a project, when budgeting, you would not know the actual costs of telephone, computers (hardware, software and maintenance) and so forth. So any numbers which subsequently come in would be at a variance.

Using a standard cost

Given that obtaining and analysing the actual payroll data is not likely, there needs to be an alternative approach. It is probable that your accounts department will have calculated standard costs for employees. A standard cost is one that takes into account the additional elements such as those listed above and comes up with a calculated average cost of employing a person, probably by role/position in the business.

An employee has a role, a role will have a salary banding, and from this it is possible to derive the average cost per role.

In preparing budget information, realistic figures for each role can be used in the budget. For example: the standard cost for the project manager above would be:

$$£59,390/252 \text{ days} = £238 \text{ per day.}$$

If calculated against the revenue-earning days in a consultancy business (see the resource planning examples), then it would be:

$$£59,390/141 = £421 \text{ per day.}$$

So, in budgeting for a project, the revenue per day to run the consulting organisation would need to be considerably in excess of £421 per day. This £421 only covers the cost of the project manager, not his team back at the office, the management infrastructure or other functions that you would expect to see.

Internal IT department

The internal IT department may prefer to calculate costs based on the productive days. You will see from the resource planning examples that there are about 200 productive days in a year. So the cost per day would be:

$$£59,390/200 = £297 \text{ per day.}$$

Taking an average additional amount of 50% on basic salary, the project would show:

Project and Programme Accounting

Role	Basic salary	Plus 50%	Per day (/252)
Project manager	£40,000	£60,000	£238
Programme director	£50,000	£75,000	£297
Consultant	£35,000	£52,500	£208
Technical	£30,000	£45,000	£179

In order to get this implemented as accepted practice within your organisation, you will need to:

1. agree with your finance director the average cost per day by role/position in the business
2. set up in the project accounting system, and also in your activity planning tool, particular roles and their associated cost per day
3. develop the budget in days and allocate each activity to a role (or roles)
4. with the number of days by role, multiply that by the day rate to give a total cost.

Budget

Activity	Days	Role	Cost per day	Total cost
Project initiation meeting	1	Project manager	£238	£238
Write initiation document	2	Project manager	£238	£476
Prepare project plan	1	Project manager	£238	£238
Install software	1	Technical	£179	£179
	5			£1131

So now we have a total in days and money.

When tracking the actual data, ensure that for each employee they are assigned a role. If a person performs more than one role, then you need to allocate roles at the entry level on the timesheet.

Actual data

Activity	Days	Role	Cost per day	Total cost
Project initiation meeting	1.00	Project manager	£238	£238
Write initiation document	1.75	Project manager	£238	£416
Prepare project plan	1.25	Project manager	£238	£298
Install software	0.50	Technical	£179	£90
	4.50			£1042

Comparison

Activity	Budget cost	Actual cost	Variance
Project initiation meeting	£238	£238	£0
Write initiation document	£476	£416	-£60
Prepare project plan	£238	£298	£60
Install software	£179	£90	-£89
			(£89.00)

Advantages of this approach

Unlike the previous approach, that relied on actual information and its lack of timeliness, you can now:

1. present figures without needing to wait for month end, year end or other financial period constraints – they are all standard costs so can be calculated immediately
2. not have to worry about security of payroll data
3. report irrespective of minor differences in salary or reward package
4. have no increased analysis required from pensions, holiday pay, sick pay or other items.

Note that by agreeing with the financial director that the standard costs are acceptable, there will be no problems with acceptance of the validity of information.

At some point you may wish to look at the standard cost and check that it reconciles back (at a high level, possibly) with the actual costs.

Subcontractors

These are the individuals whom the PAYE employees think are paid too much. Earning three times as much as your normal employee, they are an expense that the project could do without. Sound familiar?

In storing details about the resources working on a programme or project, it is better to separate out the subcontractors.

Unlike the employee, where sensitivity of payroll, overhead and holiday costs and other items will make it difficult to calculate the daily cost, with subcontractors you agree a daily or an hourly rate and then receive invoices for work performed.

The question is whether to cost by role (as for the PAYE employees) or separate out the invoiced cost from the subcontractor. A little subjective judgement is required. If the values were not significantly different for the subcontractors' day rate compared to the employees' standard cost, then I would not separate them out. The work required to do so would add little value to the final reporting figures.

Revenue recognition

The value and mechanism for producing revenue are dependent on the nature of the contract negotiation.

With a time and materials contract, it will be invoiced as the work is performed. For a fixed-price contract, it is likely that there will be payments made on delivery, probably split into a number of deliverables across the whole contract.

Revenue recognition is covered in the chapter on receivables. (See page 53.)

Reporting actual against budget

In budgeting time by activity, you are able to report the actual amount against the budget. Furthermore, with a strong design in place, it is possible to ensure that there is a consistency of data. The reporting of data and its analysis are covered in more depth in the reporting chapter. (See page 123.)

Reconciliation

At the end of each year there should be a reconciliation of the standard cost with the actual costs incurred. This would be a finance function (due to the sensitivity of the data). It needs to take place to ensure confidence is maintained in using the standard cost per day. More details on this can be found in the Expense chapter.

Expenses

In budgeting for expenses, the aim is to understand what additional expenses might be incurred on a programme or project. From this, you need to recover them, if possible, from the client.

The budgeted figure will be a total. Breaking this down between rail fares, mileage, subsistence, parking and so forth, is not practical. What is important when the programme or project is under way, is the analysis of the type of expense, and where it is not recovered, what the total cost has been. (See page 85.)

Contingency and tolerance

The PRINCE2 methodology recognises the concept of tolerance. Tolerance is the deviation from the project plan in terms of time, cost and quality.

I would suggest it is a good programme manager and a good project manager who manage to get as much contingency and tolerance into the project or programme as possible.

What is the difference?

Tolerance

'Tolerance is the permissible deviation from a Stage or Project Plan without bringing the deviation to the attention of the Project Board (or higher authority if the deviation is at project level). Separate tolerance figures should be given for time and cost.'[1]

For example, in a project or programme there may be a cost tolerance of +10%. This gives an additional 10% to spend without the need to refer to the project board.

The budgeting process should give a level of tolerance in days. Using standard costing for employees this can be converted into a value figure.

---

1. *Managing Successful Projects with PRINCE2*, OGC, ISBN 0-11-330855-8

Contingency

'In the Management of Risk, a Contingency Plan is one answer to the question "What do we do if this risk occurs?". Where a serious risk exists, the Project Board may require the Project Manager to create a Contingency Plan and add the necessary budget for it – only to be used if the risk occurs.'[2]

For the purposes of budgeting, we need to take into account what happens when a risk occurs. There might be a financial implication which has to be paid for. So in looking at the budgeting process, we need a contingency figure as well as a tolerance figure.

So how does this affect budgeting?

When negotiating a budget, calculate the total cost and revenue. Then add your 10% (or whatever, for tolerance). Now take this total and ask for a contingency amount (or hide the contingency in the initial budget) to cover the risk.

By having a standard cost, you can identify an amount for the programme which can be aligned to PAYE employee costs.

Where is this information stored?

Parkinson's Law states that work fills the time available. It is better not to show the tolerance or contingency amounts (or days) which can be drawn down. If it is there, someone will want to use it.

Instead, store the contingency and tolerance in separate project budget lines. This way, you can track the time used separately. From a programme perspective, the values can be 'rolled up' into the programme to give the total view.

A hint to consider is to create a number of contingency entries in a project. For example, a contingency for capital items, a contingency for subcontracting costs, a contingency for miscellaneous items, and an overall contingency.

Mapping to capital expenditure sign-off

In analysing the data, you need to model it based on your own criteria. In addition, when creating a budget, if a mechanism exists to map the structure to the customer's approach, subsequent reports can be produced which ease comparison on their side.

Internal IT departments

Many organisations use the concept of a capital expenditure form to get the approval to proceed with a major piece of work. If your organisation does the same, then it is worthwhile working out how to map the project and programme cost budget to the capital expenditure form. Subsequent reporting back against a capital expenditure form will be easier, and reduce the overhead of managing the financial stakeholders who keep an eye on this information.

The programme view

At project level, individual activities are identified but, by giving the project manager

---

2. *Managing Successful Projects with PRINCE2*, OGC, ISBN 0-11-330855-8

scope to define their levels of activity, method of cost estimation and tracking progress, you could lose a common view across different projects.

Our aim is to provide good management information across multiple projects. If programme management is being used for portfolio management to run the business (remember the runners/repeaters/strangers example in the introduction) then this is even more important.

The relationship between projects is based on the type of work, and not necessarily because the projects are in the same programme.

Here is the challenge: to introduce a standard coding structure for project plans at a sufficient level of consistency to enable cross-project analysis. To do this it is likely that you will need to develop a coding structure which maps project activities to methods of recording data. This is not an insignificant task but one which should pay dividends in the future.

Negotiating the budget

In presenting the estimates, these have to be accepted by all parties as realistic. Too high and the deal might be lost or the programme or project not considered economic. Too low and it could look not credible. Delivering against a tight budget will be difficult.

Roger Dawson, in the audio programme 'The secret of power negotiation', asks the question 'How much does it cost to buy a jumbo jet?'. The answer is:

10 cents per passenger mile.

The point is, that by breaking numbers down into small values, they do not appear to be so high.

So, when preparing your budget, break down the time into activities. There is a line to be drawn between micro activity planning (every hour) and weekly or monthly planning. Nevertheless, small numbers are difficult to negotiate against. (This does, of course, assume that you have sufficient detail to do some bottom-up budgeting.)

Likewise, do not send the budget to the person who will be paying (internally to a company, the budget holder; or externally, a client), instead walk through the approach. Agree with them that your activities are representative.

Operational hints and tips

1. Be very careful when you work with a client who says: 'It's all right, we will work it out at the end'. The value of goods and services diminishes soon after they are received. Again I refer to Roger Dawson in 'The secrets of power negotiation'. He makes the point that 'Prostitutes always ask for the money up front!' Always agree the budget up front.

2. Tolerance is useful. Contingency should be in there. Try to get a financial contingency budget on top of the tolerance. For both, suggest percentage figures, not values. Percentages are small numbers; values can be frightening.

3. Your own team may want to give time away – the 'It's all right, I will do this for free' throwaway comment. They will want to be seen as having the authority to make such a decision or just do not wish to confront a client. One method is to train those in 'higher authority' to use statements like 'I would like to help you. It is just that I have a project director who is unreasonable about these things'.

4. Many commercial organisations are able to reclaim the VAT on invoices raised. However, for some organisations such as insurance companies and other financial services businesses, this is not always the case. This is an important consideration to remember and find out when quoting. Your figures will look nearly one fifth higher (17.5%) for a business which cannot claim back the VAT as opposed to one which can.

5. In a services business, the project management time and programme management time, unlike consulting, can appear to be piecemeal. It will be an hour here and there chasing issues, writing reports, etc. When budgeting, make it clear that the time is spent like this, so will be invoiced as small values (or rolled up at month end to give a total figure). On the time-recording system it is important to record all of these activities, eg, phone call to Bob Jones, email to Bob to confirm call. This level of detail supports the invoice when it finally goes out.

6. Finally, I think budgeting is a combination of an art and a science. The science is in bringing together the activities into projects and programmes. The art comes in looking at the figures and then identifying how they can be made acceptable to all parties without compromising the work as a whole.

RECEIVABLES OR SALES LEDGER

Introduction

This chapter is written for those of you who charge external organisations for your services. It covers:

a. Who is the customer and what is their credit status?
b. Raising invoices, getting paid and credit notes
c. Auditors, VAT and revenue recognition
d. Posting to the general/nominal ledger.

From a traditional accounting perspective, the customer is the company or person who receives the invoice and makes the payment in return for the goods and/or services supplied. With payment received, there is a contract in place between the customer and you.

Depending on your accounting system, the customer details will be stored in the sales ledger or the receivables management module. The details held will relate to the invoice (ie, the invoice address) and may not relate to the site or person you are working with on a day-to-day basis.

At first sight, you might think that the objective is to raise collectable invoices. Certainly, the cash is important. However, you will also want the revenue on your profit and loss account and to be sure that there is no further work which has to be performed but cannot be charged for. (Otherwise costs are still being incurred with no revenue to cover them.)

The reporting from a financial system is based on the customer (for debtor analysis) and on the nominal code analysis in the general ledger. This will not normally give you sufficient detail or flexibility for a programme of projects. Indeed, it might prove a nightmare to get proper financial information out for your project.

Customers

Thinking back to the design, you will want to identify the customer. In the sales ledger the customer will be shown as the legal entity to which the invoice is addressed.

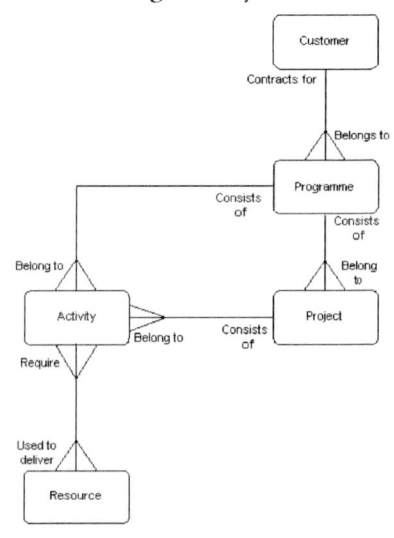

The customer might be for a programme, or just for a project. Remember that the accounting system is unlikely to understand the concept of projects or programmes unless there is a specific project accounting module installed; something to check with your finance department.

For the purposes of evaluating across projects and programmes, the system must allow you to bring together customers. This could be done through a classification code on the customer record, or analysis at transaction level. Nevertheless, check with your accounts department on what techniques are available for your system.

What is their creditworthiness?

I once heard the saying 'A sale is not a sale until the money is in the bank'. In a sales-driven company, the sale has been made when the purchase order is received, so just go and get the money in! It might not appear important at the start of the project or programme with the euphoria of making the sale but, nevertheless, you need to understand the financial state of the customer.

When a new customer is identified, the accounts department will run a credit check report with an organisation like Dun & Bradstreet. As a project or programme manager you should get a copy of the full company analysis. It is worth reading the report in its entirety.

The payments terms, which are written into a contract, should reflect the creditworthiness of the customer. If they are in financial trouble, then getting invoices paid will be enormously difficult. All sorts of delaying tactics can be used by the customer to spoil the relationship and make your own cash management difficult.

By reading the full credit report on the prospective customer you will find out such information as:

- the directors of the company
- what other directorships they hold
- the legal structure of the business
- its past few years' financial trading information.

This is valuable information. When talking with the customer, a little 'name dropping' about the directors shows that you have done your homework. Furthermore, if there are problems, you will know whom to turn to in the last resort of going above the head of your contact. (And they will be aware of this, too!)

Invoicing
Raising the invoice

The process of raising an invoice is dependent on the type of contract negotiated and how the data is captured to support the legitimacy of the invoice.

In the budgeting chapter I proposed that you should align budget, project plan and timesheet capture at activity level. As the work is performed, you need to reconcile:

- What was the budget versus the actual?
- What was planned versus what has been performed?

Project and Programme Accounting

and then find the data in your systems to support the invoice! However, it is not always easy to collect the information.

For example, without a rigorous policy of weekly timesheet entry, the actual/comparative analysis cannot be made. On a project with 10 people, each day represents 10 working days; taking 5 productive days per week (ignoring holidays, sickness and so forth which are covered later in advanced resource planning) the numbers soon add up.

5 x 10 = 50 days per week
50 x £900 per day (consultancy rate) = £45,000 in revenue.

If invoicing is linked to deliverable and you are not sure of the deliverable status (due to late timesheets and supporting documentation not up to date), then an invoice and its subsequent payment are delayed.

Where will the data come from for invoicing?

You need to identify in your organisation how data is fed into the sales invoicing cycle. In the structure below, there are 5 different classes of resource against the activities in the project or programme.

Programme & Project Invoicing

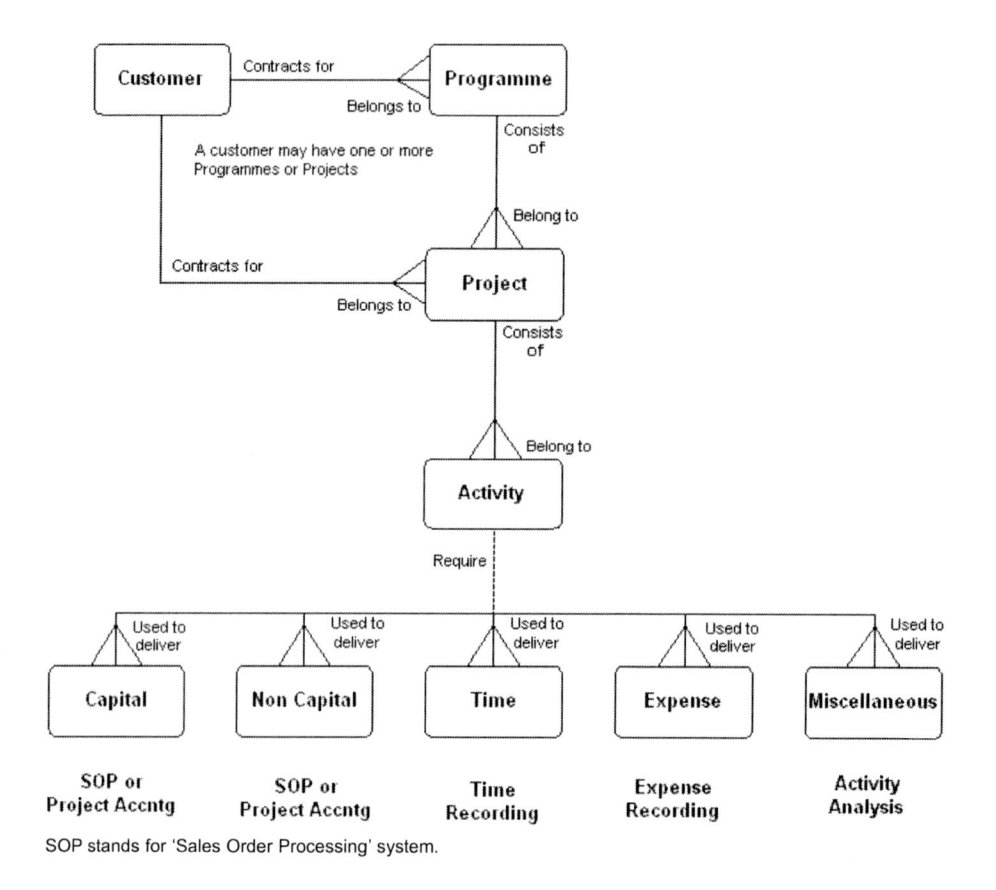

```
                Contracts for
     Customer ─────────────────◁ Programme
              └─ Belongs to ───┘      △
                                      │ Consists
     A customer may have one or more  │   of
     Programmes or Projects           │
                                      │ Belong to
                                      △
     Contracts for
     ──────────────────────────◁ Project
              └─ Belongs to ───┘      △
                                      │ Consists
                                      │   of
                                      │ Belong to
                                      △
                                   Activity
                                      ┊
                                   Require
```

	Used to deliver	Used to deliver	Used to deliver	Used to deliver	Used to deliver
	Capital	Non Capital	Time	Expense	Miscellaneous
	SOP or Project Accntg	SOP or Project Accntg	Time Recording	Expense Recording	Activity Analysis

SOP stands for 'Sales Order Processing' system.

'Project Accntg' represents a specific project accounting system as part of a main enterprise resource planning (ERP) system.

For the receipt of revenue, the distinction between 'Capital' items and 'Non-Capital' items is to make it easier to relate to the capital expenditure form. Remember this is only for guidance; the customer may be taking all the costs (except perhaps items such as software maintenance) as capital items, including the consulting services.

Capital items

The activity analysis of work performed should tell you what has been delivered/installed. In Microsoft Project these would be the resources shown as 'Materials'.

The value to be invoiced is likely to be held in the sales order processing (SOP) module of your accounting system or in the project accounting module. It is from SOP that part of your company's order book can be calculated showing orders received but not invoiced. If you are using a project accounting module which is part of the accounting system, the capital items could be held there.

To get an invoice raised is normally a case of asking the accounts department to do so (of course, saying what can be invoiced against the contract).

Non-capital items

Like its counterpart, capital items, the activity analysis of work performed should tell you what has been delivered and/or installed.

Note that there is not necessarily an automatic link between the work being performed and the production of the invoice. The sales order processing system is unlikely to be linked to the time-recording module. Some manual intervention will be required.

Time and expenses

The time and expense recording system will capture what it says – time and expenses. By aligning activities from contract terms through budgeting, to planning, and then recording the actual values, it should be possible to report on the work that has been performed and can be invoiced. The alternatives could be:

- If the project and/or programme is fixed-price with stage payments, then out of the system could come a one-line invoice with a total figure.
- If the project and/or programme is time and materials, and justification of work performed is required, then an invoice might need a line per day or part thereof of consultancy.

For either of these, the timesheets will require review and approval before invoicing takes place.

Note that the balance of days sold against days performed calculated in the time-recording system will give you an outstanding order book for consultancy.

Miscellaneous

Again, your activity analysis should tell you what has been used as the project progresses. The difficulty with this one is that there is unlikely to be a prior record in the sales order processing system of what can be invoiced.

For example, consider you have a project and have agreed to use your training facilities, for a fixed fee per day, as the customer cannot provide their own. Unless there is a mechanism in your business for tracking the use of a room, then no paperwork will be generated to prompt you to raise an invoice.

In Microsoft Project these could be set up as 'Materials' in the 'Resource' sheet and then, when reviewing the project progress, a note (email perhaps) is sent to your accounts department asking them to raise an appropriate invoice. Alternatively, in the project accounting module, or sales order processing system, the use of rooms could be created as line items. When reviewing what is to be billed, the entry already exists ready to be released for invoicing.

Summary

So, consider for your business where the data will come from, and what processes are in place to ensure invoices are raised.

Who will be raising invoices?

In working with large organisations, there may be a number of different sales being made to different parts of the business. Your project or programme might be just one of a number of items which will be invoiced and sent for payment.

If you want to manage the relationship and perform the credit control function you will want to avoid the credit control team ringing the customer to chase payment of invoices. To prevent this occurring, make it clear to credit control that you will be chasing invoices for your project or programme.

Furthermore, be clear about who has the authority to invoice for your programme or project. You do not want an invoice being sent early, or incorrectly, due to an administrative mistake.

What to put on the invoice?

The layout and content of an invoice are important. One single invoice for a large amount of money may be delayed; not because it is wrong, but because the signatory might have a psychological block on paying out so much. Excuses, such as small errors which require complete crediting and re-invoicing, are annoying and waste time.

It is worthwhile considering raising separate invoices; one for the capital items, one for non-capital items and one or more for consultancy. Splitting out the consultancy work with dates, names and description of work (this would need to be stored on the time-recording system) will reduce any 'confusion' in the customer's mind.

For a project or programme the number of lines on the invoice for consultancy could be significant if each is stated individually. For example, on a 2,000-day project, are you going to print each consultant's name, date and summary of work? Assuming that each entry takes 2 lines and there are 25 detail lines on an invoice page, this would produce

80 invoice pages. Of course, there is a trade-off here. Sending a separate schedule to support the invoice (perhaps electronically such as emailing an Microsoft Excel extract from the time-recording system) will reduce the size of the invoice (in number of pages) but nevertheless give the same information.

Once the days have been invoiced, check that there is a way of reconciling timesheets to invoices in your system. Certainly you want to know that the day has been billed. However, should a reconciliation be required, a simple invoice, or not invoiced, flag will make it difficult to check back on an invoice-by-invoice basis. Instead, ensure that the invoice number is held against each timesheet entry.

Finally, when producing the invoice, ensure that there is a mechanism for identifying it against your programme or project within the accounting system. (See 'Aged debtors' p. 52.)

Getting the cash

The credit check report will have shown that the customer has the money. Now it is necessary to prise it out of their hands and into yours. In *The Psychology of Selling*, Brian Tracy says that your opening statement should be your closing statement. In other words, every action you perform in a sale is to close the sale. The quicker you move to the close, the faster the sale.

This is a good analogy, worth applying to invoicing and cash collection. If the contract, the project and programme documentation, the quality documents and all work performed can be used to support an invoice, then it is difficult for it to be rejected.

For example:

1. The contract states that the first invoice is raised on installation of software – the capital amount of the software.
2. The software is sent to the customer by next-day or 3-day courier.
3. The software is installed and a series of quality tests run by the consultant and the customer to prove that the installation works.
4. A client visit report is written out, signed by the consultant and the customer, accepting that the work has been performed.
5. An invoice is raised for the software and sent to the customer.
6. An invoice is raised for the consultancy and sent to the customer.

If the customer states that the software was not installed properly, the relationship turns bad, and you have to go to court, your defence is the signed documentation of:

    a. Contract confirming payment terms
    b. Software delivered by courier (overnight, 3-day or whatever) with a signature on receipt
    c. Sign-off of quality tests by both parties to prove installation of work
    d. Sign-off of a client visit report confirming that the consultant was on site and the work performed to their satisfaction.

Naturally this fits in with your quality approach of doing it right first time.

Auditors

The auditors are that charming group of people who come and check our work! The whole process described above in 'Getting the cash' will give us the supporting documentation to prove the work to the auditors. Remember that auditors want to be confident that revenue is not being over-stated.

Aged debtors

The credit controller is responsible for chasing up outstanding invoices. My own preference is to get payment of invoices on the project or programme meeting agenda. Higher authority excuses (see Roger Dawson, 'The secrets of power negotiation') such as 'My finance director is bearing down on me, can you help?' assist in smoothing the path of asking for cash.

Part of the invoice process recommended that invoices were flagged in the sales ledger with your project or programme reference. An aged debtor report is by customer, but you are only interested in the invoices that relate to your project or programme. However, be aware that if there are issues in other parts of the business, your programme might be drawn into problems as a political move.

Check with your accounts department as to whether they can produce a debtor analysis selected by project or programme reference. Without this, it will be necessary to work out manually which invoices belong to the programme and which do not – a time-consuming activity that should be automated.

VAT

At the bottom of the invoice will be a VAT calculation. The amount and level of VAT are dependent on HM Revenue & Customs guidelines and the Chancellor's whim. For many businesses it means adding on at the current rate of 17.5% of the net value of the item sold. When looking at the aged debtor report, the totals may be significantly higher than the project or programme revenue, because aged debtor includes VAT.

International projects and programmes have different VAT implications. At the start of the project or programme, check with your accounts department on what the VAT treatment will be. For example, the point of supply, such as if the consultancy takes place in another country, can affect the VAT rate and to whom it is paid.

It is important to remember that HM Revenue & Customs will require paying, whether or not you have received the money from the customer!

Finally, there are some businesses, like insurance companies, who cannot reclaim the VAT; so the costs will be higher than you receive because of this. They have to pay the gross amount and cannot claim back VAT off the invoice.

Payment terms

The aged debtor report shows the number of days since the date of the invoice and the amount outstanding by customer. Normal payment terms will be 30 days from date of invoice, so the debt is usually grouped into: under 30 days, 30 to 60 days, 60 to 90 days, over 90 days.

In the contract, it is important that payment terms are clearly indicated, and any payment you receive is then used to fund payments to suppliers (a back-to-back arrangement).

There are some accounts departments who pay invoices the month following receipt. For example:
- If an invoice is received on 30 June, this will be paid by 31 July.
- If the same invoice is received on 1 July, it will not be paid until 31 August.

Tightening your own procedures and invoicing 2 days before the end of the month, as opposed to the last working day, could improve the project or programme cash flow considerably.

Gaining commitment

Let us imagine the following scenario:

- The project started in good faith.
- The project initiation document was signed off.
- The software was installed successfully.
- The design consultancy performed.
- No invoices were raised on the customer for this work.
- The customer starts to get cold feet. They have not paid you for anything and have little exposure to you.
- The contract is cancelled and you end up with the choice of going to court for the money or walking away.

Once the money is handed over to you, there is considerably more commitment from the customer. They would be unlikely to get their money back from you – not least without a court battle – so will think twice when getting cold feet.

Put in the contract a clear invoicing profile, raise the invoices promptly and chase for payment.

Revenue recognition

What is revenue recognition? This is how you take the work you have performed and put it on to your profit and loss account.

By understanding the accounting principles of revenue recognition, you are able to negotiate your contracts, confident that the work can produce revenue.

For example: you make a sale of software with 30 days' implementation work. When invoicing the customer, you can either:

1. Invoice software and service at the same time (once all the 30 days' work has been performed)
   or
2. Invoice the software when it is shipped
   Invoice the installation service separately as it is performed
   (as part of the weekly invoicing cycle)
   or

3. Invoice the software when it is shipped
   Invoice the installation service in blocks of work based on deliverables.
   or
4. Invoice the software when it is shipped
   Invoice the installation service up front in full.

The important issue here is to understand when the sale becomes revenue in your profit and loss account. As a project or programme manager, you will be under pressure to produce revenue (especially for a public limited company). Yet your auditors will want to ensure that you can justify the revenue.

The auditors will use the 'Statement of principles for financial reporting' as their guide in identifying what can be taken as revenue.

Four points were given above about how the process can be defined. It cannot be assumed that, by raising an invoice, the auditors will accept this as revenue. Instead, there must be agreement reached with them; so it would be best to check on this before the programme or project starts.

Warranties and service fees

One other item for consideration is where there is income for a service that takes place over a period of time. An example of this is software and hardware maintenance. This revenue has its own special treatment, as in the following example.

- An invoice is raised for £24,000 for the annual software maintenance contract.
- The period of the contract is 12 months, from 1 June through to 31 May.
- During this time, the company is contracted to provide telephone help-line support and any software upgrades to the customer.
- There is an obligation to provide a service over a 12-month period.
- Therefore, our revenue profile must reflect the period over which the service is provided – 12 months.
- The invoice total is divided by 12 (being 12 months) to give us £2,000. This is the monthly amount that we can bring in as revenue.
- We still receive the cash benefit, being paid the £24,000 (+ VAT).

From a project or programme perspective this is important to understand. Our invoicing profile will show £24,000 in revenue for software maintenance. But in the profit and loss account, there will be £2,000 in the first month, with £22,000 deferred.

Revenue recognition summary

The way in which revenue is recognised onto the profit and loss account will have significant impact on your business. If you are delivering projects or programmes where revenue is based on deliverables, there will be pressure to obtain sign-off and align the deliverable dates with financial reporting dates.

Do not underestimate the impact of the other stakeholders in your business. They will want to ensure that the company's financial performance is delivered and are not likely to be interested in your programme or project problems.

Credits
Overview of credit notes
Credits are more than an annoyance. Incorrect invoicing makes it difficult for you to collect the cash, wastes time and will irritate the customer. Furthermore, credits reduce reported revenue.

It must be your objective to raise collectable invoices. The work being performed should be substantiated at all times with proof of quality delivery. A negotiated settlement where work is not charged for (being credited back) can have a significant impact on net profit. For example:

Consultancy revenue	£5,000
Cost (direct & indirect)	£4,500
Net profit (at 10%)	£500

The customer complains about some of the work and 50% of the £5,000 has to be credited. Our costs have still been incurred so our profit is not £250 but:

Consultancy revenue	£2,500
Cost (direct & indirect)	£4,500
Net profit (loss)	(£2,000)

To recover our original position we need to produce another £25,000 in revenue because £25,000 @ 10% gives us £2,500 in net profit. Our loss was £2,000 and our previous reported net position was £500.

Profit improvements through credit note analysis
It is well worthwhile analysing the reason for credit notes and to look for patterns. Remembering that programme management can be used to manage multiple projects across multiple customers, finding individual credit notes by customer is unlikely to give a view across all projects.

In the design section we identified the need for a system of common reporting through standard activities and project definitions.

Let us assume that the credit analysis codes are:

- Software failure
- Consultancy
- Chasing payment

and when entering in a credit, our credit line is the activity code of the original work.

After 6 months you can analyse credits (through SQL reporting) across customers by common activity code by credit reason. The analysis shows that credits are due to a failure to install the software correctly. Management effort can be focused on improving this service – or cease to perform it. If you improve the delivery of the service, the costs remain the same, but the revenue increases.

Credit notes and subcontractors
Here is something to consider. In working with subcontractors, you will be paying them less than you receive. What do you do if there is a credit note raised? Do you seek to get a credit out of the subcontractor if they have failed?

In taking a mark-up on the subcontractor's day rate, there is an element of risk assumed by the organisation. Risk and reward are the alchemy of the capitalist system.

I would suggest that if the values are small, then do not seek to recover them from the subcontractor. Maintaining the relationship with a subcontractor is important. However, where the values are material, try to work with the subcontractor on a mutually agreeable way forward. Individuals are unlikely to have large reserves to pay out from, so a gesture from them, such as reduced day rates, is more likely to happen.

Credit notes and utilisation
The production of the credit note may well be outside of the time-recording system. However, the calculation of the utilisation rates is in the analysis of timesheet data. These two need to be linked. (See page 69 for details on calculating the days available and utilisation.)

The 'Revised utilisation calculation' in the resource planning and utilisation examples chapter explains how there can be only 141 revenue earning days (page 110).

Where there are credits raised, each line item on a credit note needs to store the information about:
- who did the work
- the activity being performed
- for which project and/or programme
- the number of days to be credited.

The calculation of utilisation can then be performed taking this into consideration. It might provide an interesting insight into what is really going on.

Grants and matched funding
I mention this under the receivables section as, for some businesses, this is how they obtain their income.

Grants for projects can be provided by organisations such as central government or the EEC. Examples could be the provision of training courses to disadvantaged groups, or capital refurbishment projects such as building refurbishment.

The grant may be made in advance, or payment given from the provider when the work is completed. In the latter example, this will create a negative cash flow which must be funded until the project is completed.

Another method is 'matched funding'. Here an organisation will receive a grant of money on the condition that, for every £ given, the business puts in a £ (or some other relationship between the two). For example, suppose that a not-for-profit organisation is promised £10,000 in income, if they match this pound for pound. Here the total project value would be £20,000, with half coming from an external organisation.

The important point is to understand what income is coming, from where and when.

General ledger postings

The general ledger or nominal ledger will contain a summary of the revenue that has been raised and costs which are incurred.

You may be asking, 'Why not just store in the general ledger all the revenue analysis codes for the project or programme?' The reality is that this would make the chart of accounts unwieldy.

For example: you are a software supplier who sells software with 25 separate modules. Each module comes with software maintenance.

The implementation could be analysed at activity level through 20 different activity codes. Now, instead of three lines saying, in the chart of accounts:

- software revenue
- maintenance revenue
- consultancy revenue

we have 70 lines (25 for software, 25 for maintenance and 20 for consultancy). Our interest in these is important but has little relevance to other parts of the organisation. So the requirement is to analyse out the individual activities, and their mapping to the general ledger.

Schematically this could be:

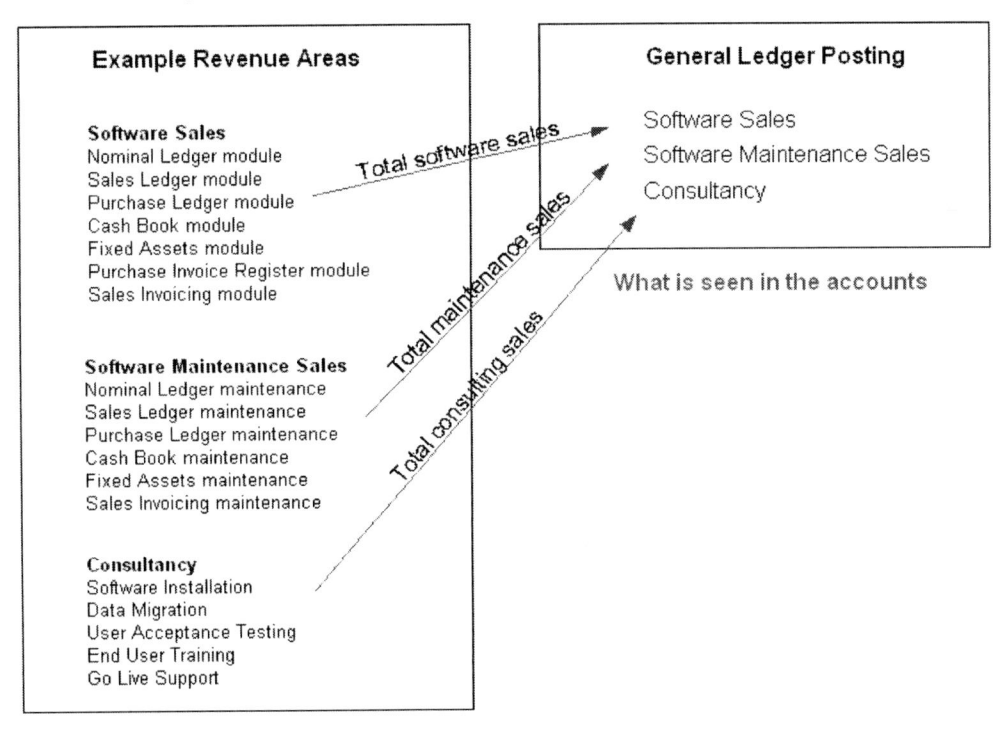

Example Revenue Areas

Software Sales
Nominal Ledger module
Sales Ledger module
Purchase Ledger module
Cash Book module
Fixed Assets module
Purchase Invoice Register module
Sales Invoicing module

Software Maintenance Sales
Nominal Ledger maintenance
Sales Ledger maintenance
Purchase Ledger maintenance
Cash Book maintenance
Fixed Assets maintenance
Sales Invoicing maintenance

Consultancy
Software Installation
Data Migration
User Acceptance Testing
End User Training
Go Live Support

General Ledger Posting

Software Sales
Software Maintenance Sales
Consultancy

Total software sales →
Total maintenance sales →
Total consulting sales →

What is seen in the accounts

What we see in the Programme / Project Analysis

Hints and ideas

1. Credit control may be wary of sharing any information with you. I spoke with a project manager who was going to visit a client. He asked his credit control department what invoices were outstanding. Instead of forwarding this information, there was a flat response: 'What is it to you?' You may need to explain to credit control that you are there to help.
2. Raising invoices for small amounts is worth pursuing. It is a psychological issue, as stated earlier, especially in the consulting business where the value of services can appear to diminish as time passes.
3. Try suggesting payment by direct debit. I have yet to meet a financial director who is keen on this idea, but it is worth a try. (If nothing else, it should raise a smile when you suggest it.)
4. Get the customer to book and pay for hotels and flights directly. There is no money to be made from this, only the administrative headache of claiming back the expense. If you have been re-invoicing these expenses, then your overall programme or project revenue will go down, but the margin, as a % of total turnover, will rise.
5. For a first step, get your credit note analysis in order. Even if it does not align with activities, make a start with the reason codes. Only when some data is available can the analysis begin and an action plan commence.
6. When negotiating a contract, try and get a large deposit payment prior to doing any work. This will help your cash flow and show commitment from the customer.
7. When starting a project, check where invoices should be sent. For example, I worked with an organisation once who had multiple sites. The project manager had a desk at 2 sites. He asked that invoices be sent to the accounts department, who then took 7 to 10 days to put them in the internal post to him. After 2 weeks, he received them, and if there was a query, then it would be nearly 3 weeks before I found out.

PAYABLES/PURCHASE LEDGER

Introduction

Within a project or programme it is necessary to track expenditure with outside organisations. The supplier may provide software, hardware or services. Services could be subcontracted consultancy.

The need is to track the costs incurred, make payment and, from a corporate perspective, analyse the costs incurred across multiple projects and programmes.

Yet, for many businesses, analysis is at the supplier and product levels, not for a specified project or programme of projects. Without this level of detail, it will be difficult to analyse the project or programme costs, for the data is lost in the depths of the purchase order processing system.

The accounting view

Before discussing the esoteric issues of project and programme accounting, I will look at the typical life cycle.

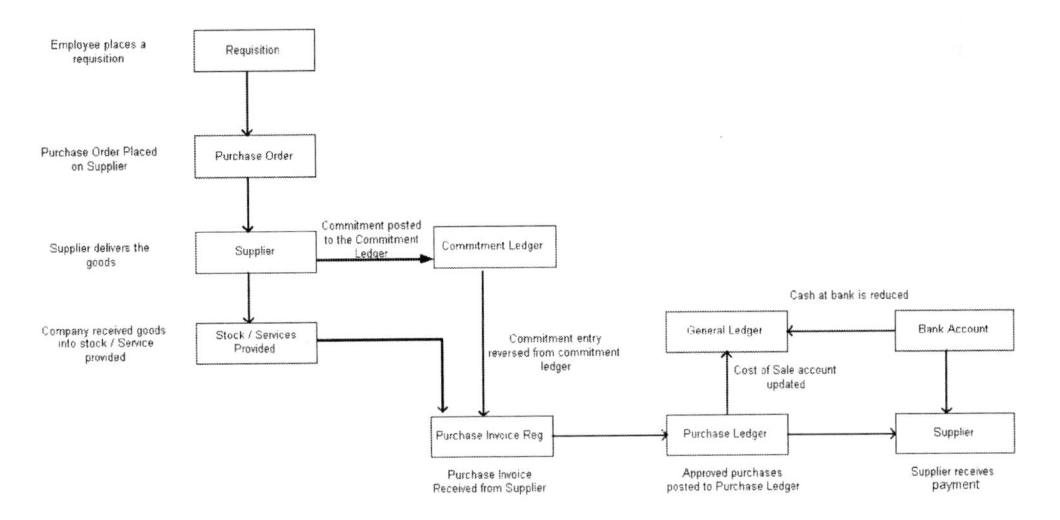

1. An employee places a requisition. Not all organisations use requisition forms. This may be as simple as an email to the purchasing officer, or a telephone call.
2. A purchase order is raised and placed on a supplier. In some organisations there may be a verbal order. To track the value and content of what is being purchased, it is better to enforce the discipline of getting a purchase order written out, or prepared in an electronic ordering/e-procurement system. Purchase orders are written out to a supplier which are likely to cover many departments as a summation of requisitions.
3. The supplier delivers the goods which are received into stock. In the case of services, a subcontractor will provide consultancy. For items such as room hire (for meetings) this usage may occur without paperwork because there is no goods receipting. The only paperwork then is a purchase invoice.
4. To show that the company has made a commitment to expenditure, an entry is posted to the commitment ledger. This normally happens when the delivery is made.

Project and Programme Accounting

Check with your accounts department whether they perform commitment accounting. I have heard some organisations use the concept of soft and hard commitments. A soft commitment is where the purchase order is placed but goods not received. The hard commitment is where the goods are received. The posting of the soft commitment is reversed when the hard commitment entry is made.

5. The purchase invoice register is updated when the purchase invoice is received. At this point the commitment is reversed from the commitment ledger. The purchase invoice will normally go through an approval process prior to payment being made. This approval could require a signatory or checking against the goods received note.
6. The purchase ledger is updated with the purchase invoice details. It will show that the supplier now has a credit amount against them.
7. The cost of sale account is updated in the general ledger.
8. Finally, when the invoice is approved and payment made, money is taken from the bank account. The amount shown as a credit on the supplier account is reduced to zero.

In medium to large organisations, this takes place typically through a purchasing department who will be placing orders on many suppliers. The orders placed will be for many departments in the organisation. Contract terms are negotiated on a company, not project or programme, basis.

Project and programme requirements

The details described above are the typical life cycle of purchase to delivery. For the project or programme the needs are to:

a) Place purchase orders on one or more suppliers and receive goods from supplier(s) by project and/or programme. In grouping like items together in the purchasing department, the individual analysis is lost. There needs to be a mechanism to flag a purchase order line by project code or programme code, so check if this is possible within the constraints or your current systems. If it is not, then you will need to keep a separate list of purchase orders raised for your project and/or programme.

b) Make part and full payment at a project level to the supplier.

The distinction by programme and project will need to be recognised by the supplier. One project may have problems with the delivery, while another will not. Ensure that you sign off delivery on the goods receipting based on acceptable quality or whatever the criteria are. In the section below, on payment, there is a discussion about managing cash and suppliers. It is better if you can get the cash from the customer before you have to pay your supplier.

The challenges are:

c) When the delivery is a service, perhaps subcontracting consultancy, then the goods received note is replaced by a timesheet.

Now, the time-recording system will need to record this information. It is unlikely that you will want to record it twice – a separate entry in the commitment ledger – so we need to ensure that subcontracted consultancy performed, but no invoice received from the contractor yet, is shown as a commitment. To achieve this would require a report at the end of each reporting period (weekly, monthly) to post one line to a commitment account of work performed by contractors but invoice not received. In an organisation which buys in subcontractor time and sells it on, there is a danger that the sales invoice is raised, and the cost of the time not shown in the cost entry of the profit and loss account (because no invoice was received). To overcome this, an adjustment journal should be posted to show the liability until such time as the invoice is received from the subcontractor.

Without the project-level analysis, it will not be possible to 'roll up' costs to a programme level. Cross-project and programme analysis is lost.

Payment

Payment will require cash. The considerations for internal IT departments, against those who are selling services, are different, although in either case, maximising the best terms from the supplier is always good business practice.

Internal IT departments

When putting in place a contract, you want to get the best payment terms for the project or programme. This will help the cash finances and your organisation as a whole. For example, on a £100,000 purchase you might want to only pay a small deposit, on delivery another tranche, with a retention in place until the system is signed off as accepted.

Description	Paid to supplier £	Supplier %
Deposit	£10,000	10%
Amount on delivery	£40,000	40%
30 days later	£20,000	20%
Retention	£20,000	20%
Totals	£100,000	100.00%

IT services business

In this instance it is assumed that you are purchasing software and services to re-sell on to a customer. So, when putting in place a contract, you want to get the payment to the supplier on a back-to-back basis with the customer. Even better would be to get payment from the customer, but only give a part payment to the supplier.

For example, on a £100,000 software sale to the customer, where you are making £20,000 (20%) in margin, your payment profile could be:

Description	Paid to supplier £	Supplier %	Received from customer £	Customer %
Deposit	£10,000	12.50%	£20,000	20%
Amount on delivery	£50,000	62.50%	£70,000	70%
Retention	£20,000	25.00%	£10,000	10%
Totals	£80,000	100.00%	£100,000	100.00%

(The ideal is to get 100% on delivery from the customer and no retention.)

Again, when negotiating at a company level, the terms are for the business as a whole. This could adversely affect the project cash flow but benefit the organisation as a whole.

Purchasing controls for projects and programmes

When implementing a purchasing system, business controls need to be in place to ensure that no orders are placed, or payments made, without proper authority.

In implementing the controls for a project or programme system, consider the following:

1. Purchase orders are raised as one per project or programme, not across multiple projects. It makes tracking them easier by project.
2. Ensure that all purchase orders are signed by the project or programme manager.
3. If the project manager has some authority to sign purchase orders, consider if there should be a value limit to their sign-off before it is referred to the programme manager.
4. The analysis of the item lines on a purchase order match back to the project costing. Where projects are of a like type (remember the runners/repeaters/strangers, page 4), try to bring a consistency to order lines. It is then possible to perform cross-project analysis.
5. Payment terms must be stated on purchase orders and are consistent with the cash flow forecast.
6. Goods, when delivered, must be signed off for quality, not just signed for and therefore accepted on delivery.
7. If the delivery is a service, then the subcontractor must complete a timesheet. Clarify how you handle off-site work where there is no visibility of the subcontractor's activities.
8. Subcontractors' timesheets must be attached to their purchase invoice. These must match the timesheets entered into the system and should be consistent with the activity-level analysis. If possible, get the subcontractor to post entries in to your time-recording system like any other employee. In this way the time is tracked immediately. Expenses should be entered in the same way.
9. Payment to the supplier should be on a back-to-back basis with payment from the customer.
10. Only pay subcontractors based on the deliverable (such as a PRINCE2 product) rather than just on work performed.
11. If the item is being delivered to a remote site (and perhaps signed off by one of your own personnel) check if your goods receipting system can be published in a Web environment (or through something like Citrix). In this way, there could be an updating of your own system as soon as receipting takes place.
12. Once you have a reasonable data set and can analyse spend across multiple projects and programmes, look at how you can work with your suppliers to get a better deal, therefore reducing costs.

Note: It is not always necessary to automate the production of purchase orders. They could be written out manually if this is more efficient.

Reporting

In the software requirements chapter, there is a section on reporting on costs (page 145).

Conclusion

In purchasing, it is important that there is control of expenditure. By developing a purchasing system design based on the hierarchy of projects and programmes it will be possible to provide cross-programme and project analysis as well as efficiently track costs for your own programme or project.

CASH

Introduction

In any business, running out of cash is disastrous: cash is king. So, you need to manage the cash flow within the project and programmes.

The size of the project will make a difference when considering cash flow forecasting. For small projects of only a few days' duration, then this is likely to be unnecessary overkill. However, it is important when entering into any contract to be clear on when payment will be made to suppliers, and for organisations charging for their services, when money will come in.

The chapters on accounts receivable and accounts payable touch on the issues of tracking cash flow. Here the points are brought together to give a holistic view.

For those of you who are not in a revenue-generating business, what comes in is not relevant. However, what is paid out could well be material and require forecasting for your accounts department. Finally, if your project or programme is expected to deliver significant cash benefits to the business, it may be considered a self-funding piece of work. In these instances, cash forecasting is important.

Cash flow forecast

First, you need a cash flow forecast. To prepare this you need to identify the money coming in and going out. This will be based on the activities performed, so it is likely that it can be extrapolated from the project plan. For businesses where projects and programmes are an internal function, there is unlikely to be sales, only costs.

The cash flow forecast (CFF) will look like:

Description	Month 1 £	Month 2 £	Month 3 £	Month 4 £
Coming in				
Sales (a)	£100,000	£80,000	£50,000	£125,000
Going out				
Purchases	£50,000	£70,000	£25,000	£15,000
Payroll & subcontractors	£30,000	£40,000	£40,000	£45,000
Total (b)	£80,000	£110,000	£65,000	£60,000
Bank				
Opening (c)	£150,000	£170,000	£140,000	£125,000
Net movement (d = a – b)	£20,000	(£30,000)	(£15,000)	£65,000
Closing (e = c + d)	£170,000	£140,000	£125,000	£190,000

So, in Month 1 you have £100,000 coming in, a total expenditure of £80,000, giving a net movement of £20,000; an opening bank account of £150,000 which, with the £20,000 added, as you received more than you spent; gives a closing balance of £170,000. Months 2 through to 4 are shown as examples.

This is based on cash sales (or where the cash is collected). It is an important distinction; it is not when the sales invoice is raised nor when the purchase invoice is received.

As regards sales invoices, these will be paid based on the terms of the contract. So it is particularly important that you are clear about when payment will be made. Supplier invoices will be subject to an agreement – these terms might or might not be onerous.

Improving the position

There are ways to improve the cash management and cash movements on the project or programme by breaking down the individual areas further. For example, separate out the sales by capital, non-capital and services (if that is the distinction in your business). So, your revised cash flow forecast would say:

Description
Coming in
Capital item sales
Non-capital item sales
Services
Going out
Capital item purchases
Non-capital item purchases
Payroll
Subcontractors
Expenses

Look at the profile of delivery to see if items can be installed earlier or work performed at a different pace (keeping in line with the dates for the final deliverables).

In the contract negotiation, is it worth trying to get more of a deposit up front? Should there be retention terms? If so, seek to minimise the percentage.

When paying suppliers and subcontractors, negotiate the longest payment terms. Endeavour to get a back-to-back arrangement in place. If the customer pays you on sign-off, then pay the supplier on that sign-off. For subcontractors, consider paying based on deliverable (not just work done). This makes it more in their interest to complete an item than to extend the work.

Automate the generation of a cash flow forecast

If you use a project-planning product, such as Microsoft Project, then much of the work can be automated. For example, when preparing the project plan, against the activities, assign the resources to be used. You will need fields for revenue and cost, then calculate the revenue dates (for the profit and loss account), the cost dates (also for the profit and loss account) and the expected cash receipt and cash payment dates.

In Microsoft Project there are spare fields, including date fields. Simply rename these date fields as follows (in addition to your normal start and finish dates for the activity):

Project and Programme Accounting

Field	Comment	How calculated?
Date 1 becomes: *Revenue date*	This is the date you expect to raise an invoice so you can put the revenue onto the profit & loss account for the delivery or activity.	The invoice is raised when the work is completed (or 'as performed' depending on the nature of the contract). If 'as performed', and we invoice weekly, the revenue date is likely to be 7 days after the finish date. From this revenue date we can derive the expected cash received date.
Date 2 becomes: *Cash received date*	This is the date you expect to get the cash, based on the invoice that was raised.	Dependent on the nature of the contract, assuming that the payment terms are 30 days from invoice date, this can be calculated as 7 + 30 days from finish date (7 from the weekly invoicing above.) Assuming, of course, that they pay on due date! Or it is the revenue date plus 30 days.
Date 3 becomes: *Cost date*	This is the date you expect to receive an invoice (if the item is from a supplier), or when the people cost will be incurred.	You can accrue in the accounts for the cost, but you need to make that accrual. The invoice may be received from the supplier quickly after the item has been received. Prudent accounting would suggest you account for this immediately.
Date 4 becomes: *Cash payment date*	This is the date you expect to pay the supplier or the employee.	These are supplier dependent. It is here that you need to investigate the issues with regard to the particular project or programme. This needs to be a configurable item based on each product or service bought in.

Notes
1. By accounting for the cost immediately from a supplier, 'Date 4' can be used also for the people cost; for once used, people will need paying.
2. The relationship with the supplier needs to be understood. Extended payment terms for some suppliers will assist in the cash flow management. For ease of calculation, it might be better to take a prudent figure (such as 14 days after the invoice received date).
3. If the revenue is taken based on deliverable stages, it will be necessary, in the resource sheet, to create material resources which are identified as stage payments with an amount. Then, in the project plan, enter the stage payment against the appropriate deliverable.

Setting up in Microsoft Project

Take an example project and use this as the baseline for developing the cash flow model. The additional fields to be defined in the task sheet are:

Default Field	New Name	Formula
Date 1 (task)	Revenue date	Finish + 7
Date 2 (task)	Cash RCV date	Revenue date + 30
Date 3 (task)	Cost date[1]	Start
Date 4 (task)	Cash pay date[2]	Cost date + 14

Notes:
1. Although the cost date and start date are synonymous, in reading any output it assists in understanding the data.
2. The cash pay date I have taken as the cost date + 14 days. If it is a payroll item, then the law of averages tells us that half the time it is in the first part of the month, and half in the last part. For payment to suppliers, 14 days is quick, so we are being prudent.

In the resource sheet we need to enter the rates to reflect the revenue earned and cost incurred.

Finally, export the data to a Microsoft Excel pivot table. You will need to edit the export map to include the additional fields. In Microsoft Excel, it is then possible to pivot on the data to produce revenue and cost profiles.

Items to watch out for
Giving away the profit figure

In creating, within the project plan, both the revenue and cost figures, this will identify the margin that you expect to receive. For those people who work with cost plus contracts this is not an issue.

However, where you have competitively tendered, and your programme plan or project plan is to be loaded onto the customer's system, do you really want them to see the margin that is expected?

In these circumstances, it is necessary to create a separate project plan with the cost figures and merge the two outputs in Excel.

Expense repayment

Out-of-pocket expenses could be a significant overhead. In the chapter on expenses (page 85), there are suggestions on how these could be recovered. Reimbursement of the employee's expenses will be done quickly, but invoicing the customer and getting paid will give a lag between cash going out and coming in.

Should this be material, then provision should be made in the forecast for this.

VAT

The cash flow forecast will be net of VAT. HM Revenue & Customs will want paying, irrespective of whether you have been paid. Check with your accounts department over the handling of VAT and how it is reclaimed and paid.

Cash receipting

You are likely to want to chase the customer for payment rather than hand this work to credit control. When money comes into a business, it is often posted against the oldest invoice first (especially when it is a lump-sum payment). I suggest that when payment is received, you ensure it is posted against your project or programme invoices.

RESOURCE PLANNING & UTILISATION

Introduction

Projects and programmes need people. How many people and their availability to work on the project or programme requires calculation. You need to understand what resources are required, and therefore what their cost will be and for those who invoice for time, the revenue they hope to achieve. This chapter explains how to calculate the number of productive days.

For those in the consulting industry, I have detailed some of the salient issues that are faced in generating revenue and resolving utilisation conflicts.

Calculating the available days
Working year

To calculate the number of working days in the year:

Description	Days	
Days in year	365	
Weekends	104	Less
Public holidays	8	Less
Working days	253	

If the project or programme is international, then the working days of the week and number of public holidays vary.

United Kingdom

In the UK the working week is Monday to Friday (except public holidays). There are 8 public holidays (or bank holidays) although, depending on the occupation of the person, these may or may not be recognised as days off.

Overseas

For some countries in the Middle East, work takes place at the weekends but not on Fridays or Thursday afternoons. I believe there are 13 days that are set aside as public holidays in France and Germany. Moreover, your calculation of working days must reflect any local customs and issues.

Activities which reduce available days

If only we could achieve 253 productive days! For a project manager or programme manager every day could deliver more successes. However, from this 253 we need to deduct time for training, holidays and, yes, people will be ill. Furthermore, there will be time spent on internal activities such as backing up PCs, having a performance appraisal and so forth, which reduce the number of days available for productive work.

Examples of days lost are:

- holidays
- sickness
- training
- performance appraisals
- technology
- departmental/company meetings
- absence
- administration

First, here is a revised model of time (the percentages are rounded for clarity).

Description	Days	% of Total
Working days	253	
Less		
Holidays	25	10%
Sickness	5	2%
Training	12	5%
Performance appraisals	2	1%
Technology	6	3%
Team/dept meetings	2	1%
Absence	1	1%
Available days	200	

Holidays
This is a variable number depending on your organisation and often different by employee, based on number of years of service and seniority.

Sickness
It is necessary to make provision for days off sick. In suggesting 5 days (see table), this does not mean that people can take 5 days off each year. Rather it is in recognition of the fact that there is illness and time will be lost. Across a team of 100 people, if each person has 3 days' sickness then 300 working days are lost.

Internal IT departments
For an IT department, if 300 days are lost through sickness, this is equivalent to 1.5 man-years of effort (where we are assuming 200 productive days per year). Planning for the delivery of a number of projects without being conscious of this fact could seriously affect what is delivered against what was expected.

IT services business
In revenue earning businesses these 300 days would equate to lost revenue. So looking at your daily rates, consider this table of lost revenue:

Average daily rate	Sickness days	Revenue not received
£800	300	£240,000
£850	300	£255,000
£900	300	£270,000
£950	300	£285,000
£1,000	300	£300,000

The impact of not budgeting for sickness could prevent you from reaching a target due to circumstances beyond your control. Public limited companies need to be especially aware of this fact, as not meeting stock market expectations can cause a fall in share price.

Training
Training is vital and an important part of future productivity and profit. Nevertheless, it also represents 'lost' days to the project or programme. You need to take into account this investment of time.

Performance appraisals
As with training, appraisal is vital and you need to budget for two days for performance appraisals, representing half a day preparation and half a day appraisal for each team member twice a year. A main appraisal should be conducted at the start of the financial year, with six-month review to ensure the objectives set are being met.

Technology
You may be using computers to help produce profit but technology of any kind needs maintenance, support and, in the case of computer data, it needs to be backed up. Furthermore, there will be new releases of software that need to be installed, systems reconfigured and other non-productive time activities.

The six days are calculated as half a day per month (4 hours) with 2 hours every other week for backing up the machine. I have chosen to ignore rebuild and new software release time in this instance. This is an investment in the security of the business.

By setting a budget for technology that covers backing, there is formal recognition of this activity, and time available for this essential work to take place. For installation of new software, or upgrades to existing systems, this is additional time and will reduce the overall productivity. I have not included this in the above model but commented on its likely impact in the consulting section below.

Departmental/company meetings
It is likely that the line manager will want to bring the team together. Companies are changing quickly as the business environment moves. So, in budgeting for the available days, take into account the time spent at departmental or company meetings.

Absence
This is to cover visits to the dentist, compassionate leave and so forth. These things will happen; if you do not allow for them, the comparative budget versus actual analysis from your system will start to become meaningless, and your budgeted targets not hit.

Revised model

Description	Days	% of Total	Class
Working days	253		
Less			
Holidays	25	10%	Non-productive
Sickness	5	2%	Non-productive
Training	12	5%	Investment
Performance appraisals	2	1%	Investment
Technology	6	3%	Investment
Team/dept meetings	2	1%	Investment
Absence	1	1%	Non-productive
Available days	200		

Note: The purpose of the 'Class' column is to define the grouping of each area. Holidays and sickness are non-productive. Activities such as training, performance appraisals and internal meetings are design to invest in the people. This is about presentation of the figures once the data has been collected. Again I have rounded the percentages for clarity.

Administration time

Here is a good way to lose time. The admin bucket will enable people to get away with not properly analysing their time. Excuses such as, 'It was general admin', will prevail. Furthermore, any attempts to limit admin time will be difficult to police. I recommend that you do not set up a project for admin time.

> **Hint:** Set up a 'waiting for project' project that a person can post their time to when there is nothing else which appears correct. Ensure that a full description of the work is put in against the timesheet entry. Most time-recording systems allow records to be moved from one project to another. This will get round the administration project and force people to identify what they were doing. From this, if there is a need for administrative work, then consider employing an administrative assistant. They will be considerably cheaper than employing your highly skilled individuals to do this work.

How long is a working day?

Depending on your industry, it will vary. What is important from a time recording, revenue and cost view is to define:

a) what half a day is
b) what a full day is
c) what a day and a quarter is
d) what a day and a half is.

Resource Planning & Utilisation

Why?
1. If you are charging for consultancy based on a daily rate, then a revenue opportunity may be lost. Consultants may work long hours (perhaps 9 or 10 hours per day). On a working day of 7.5 hours this adds another 2.5 hours (or an extra one third), which is not being recovered if it is a daily charge (as opposed to hourly).
2. The hours in a day need to be put into bands to define what day or part thereof, they fall in to.
3. When you are estimating for a project, if it is on an hourly basis, then this needs to be converted into a day.

Hours	Day equivalent
Up to 5 hours	0.5 day
5 to 9 hours	1 day
Over 9 hours	1.25 days

I met someone who said they had to 'normalise' the working hours. The consultants were working on a project, putting in a 60-hour week. This had to be 'normalised' down to 40 hours for billing purposes. The issues to answer are:

a) What is charged to the client?
b) What is the cost of the work? If there were no overtime claimed, then an hourly cost would overstate the cost when compared to the payroll costs.

In point (b) there is the 'soft' issue of overworking the consultants. Also, was the idea of the 60-hour week a part of your plan to achieve the work?

Influences to consider
Facilitator and producer objectives

In *Managing Industrial Risk** by John Woodhouse, the objectives of the producers (those who generate the wealth) are compared with the facilitators (those who are employed to support this function).

This can be applied as an analogy to the challenge of planning consultancy when working in a sales-driven organisation. For example:

Producer objectives (Sales team)	Facilitator objectives (Resource coordinator)
Increase sales figures – sell more consultancy irrespective of the number or skills of consultants	Find work for all consultants in the pool without having to worry about peaks and troughs in particular skill areas
Keep the customer happy – have consultants available at short notice	Maximise utilisation through ensuring that the consultants diaries are booked for 6 months-plus in advance
Provide high skill-level consultants – ensure only highly skilled consultants are ever booked to customers	Provide a mix of consultants to train up the more junior members of the team

* ISBN 041247590-1

Project and Programme Accounting

John Woodhouse makes the point: 'Sadly one cannot achieve all these attractive goals at the same time'.

In planning it is necessary to identify the different objectives and seek to manage round them.

Resistance from TOTO

TOTO stands for Top Of The Organisation. In preparing the resource availability model, you are likely to encounter resistance from TOTO if they do not understand the point about days which are not available through the non-productive and investment items. Your political opponents will seek to make capital out of this. If the culture of the business is not to train people, then this will be seen as unproductive time which they consider can be put to better use – ie, working.

In negotiation there is a technique where you present small numbers. It is much harder to then negotiate against those numbers. To make the point, you need to present the full table above and question which ones are not realistic.

Hint: It might be an idea to inflate training, technology, team meetings and so forth a little. In talking with TOTO you have some room for manoeuvre. Everyone wants to feel they win in a negotiation.

Remember, you want a final budget that is realistic.

The reporting requirements

In designing the resource planning and utilisation model, it is necessary to consider the reporting hierarchy and types of reports which will be requested. Data should be easy to access and analyse to provide value to a business.

An example structure could be:

Role	Key Reporting and Analysis	Other Analysis Types
Director	Total Chargeable Days Total Revenue Revenue by Runner / Repeater / Stranger	Sales Mix - New / Existing Customers Consultancy by Market Sector
Practice Manager	Total Productive Days Non-Chargeable Days Activity Analysis Credit Note Analysis	Consultant Comparison Pre-Sales resource rqmts
Employee	Specific Project Analysis Activity Analysis Total Days Charged Total Days worked	Geographical Location Travel Time

So, in looking at the design of your system, consider the outputs needed. By working back from outputs, it will be possible to ensure the correct data is captured in the first place.

TIME RECORDING

Introduction

For those of you who do not work in a timesheet culture, this is probably your biggest challenge. Getting a person to accurately record their time and therefore account for their activities is not an insignificant challenge.

The most obvious reason to get people to account for their time is to track the actual time spent on particular project and programme activities. There are also important accounting considerations. Depending on the method of recognising revenue and costs, this could have an impact on your company's profit and loss, and balance sheet at year-end, and for those in a publicly quoted company, mid-year for the interim reporting period.

Before reading this chapter, you need to have reviewed the following:

- The 'Resource planning and utilisation' chapter (page 69), where the working year was divided up into productive, investment and non-productive time;
- The 'Design' chapter (page 15), which shows how a project consists of a number of activities;
- The 'Budgeting' chapter (page 28) where the level of granularity of activity analysis is discussed and reviewed.

This chapter completes this process through the identification of what is required to record time successfully. There is a section on what problems you could encounter, with suggestions on how these can be overcome.

Setting up a timesheet system

Time can be stored in hours and minutes, hours and decimal parts of hours, days or part days. For example, a timesheet could be entered in as:

Travel time: London to Brighton	1 hour 15 minutes
	1.25 hours
	75 minutes
	0.16 days (1.5/7.5 hours in a day)

My own preference is decimal hours. It makes the mathematics in a spreadsheet easier, and thinking in something like 6-minute time slots can become a nonsense.

So, to get your colleagues to enter their time into a time-recording system, it is a case of:

1. Create the projects
2. Create the activities against which time is to be recorded for each project
3. Get the team to enter the hours performed against each activity
4. Analyse the data.

Think about what you did last week and try to identify in 1-hour slots, what work was performed for each working day. Unless you have a mechanism for noting this as it is done, the detail is lost.

For example:

1. In a project consulting business, a consultant is on site on Monday training the client. At the end of the visit he or she fills in a written timesheet report which the customer signs. This is then used as the input document to the time-recording system.

2. If you are working on a number of projects concurrently, or perhaps are a manager of a team and want to analyse your time, then during the day, activities must be recorded as they are performed. This is the type of work I typically perform. My preference is to use a Daytimer with two pages per day. I write down a list of activities I need to do at the start of the day, then tick them off. Should something else come up, such as an email to be responded to, or a telephone call comes in, then I note this down in the list. At the end of the working day or working week, I can look at each day and see exactly what took place. If more information is needed, I look at the emails I sent. Often these are good reminders of the specifics.

Both of the above require personal discipline. If you want help with this, go into your bathroom and look at the person in the mirror!

How often to enter timesheets?

Personally I think they should be recorded weekly. In big projects, if there is a problem with a particular activity, then the recording of time will show where it is being used.

For consulting businesses, where projects can be invoiced weekly, the quicker the timesheet is in, the quicker the invoice can be raised.

Getting the timesheets entered

What is everyone's favourite radio station? WIIFM – What's In It For Me?

This applies to timesheets. What is in it for me? Very little? You accurately record every 15-minute time slot and post the timesheets religiously. Management evaluate the time, model it, graph it, and conclude that you could be more productive if you stopped talking to your colleagues, cut down on coffee breaks and, by reducing lunch hours from 1 hour to 45 minutes, the company would get an additional:

- 15 minutes per day x 5 days per week = 75 minutes per week
- 75 x 40 weeks (200 productive days/5 days per week) = 3,000 minutes per annum
- 3,000/60 = 50 hours
- 50/35 hours (working week) = 1.33 weeks
- 1.33/40 (weeks) = 3.3%

Fantastic, you now have a 3.3% productivity improvement by just cutting the lunchtime from 1 hour to 45 minutes. Scientific management, from the (Dickensian) managers' perspective, is fantastic. If only they would work longer hours then the work would be done!

This is a fallacy. If you do not relate the collection of timesheets to a person's own motivators, then you will have a significant challenge. The time entered will say what they think you want to see. It may also hide what was really going on.

What sort of motivators?
1. Personal development
a. Part of the role
In defining the job description, set one of the responsibilities as the accurate recording of their time.

At the annual appraisal and mid-year review, ensure that timesheet review is part of the process. Set an objective in the appraisal, if timesheet return is a problem, that this must improve. If there is no improvement, this is noted as a problem on their appraisal form.

b. Improving yourself
Peter F. Drucker in *The Effective Executive** makes the point that those people who actively record their time, review it and then amend their behaviour are the most productive.

If you use a Daytimer (www.daytimer.co.uk), there is a daily planning routine. At their TimePower seminars they emphasise planning time, prioritising and ensuring that you are free from distractions and interruptions.

The timesheet information is fundamental to understanding how you are performing. In introducing a timesheet system and getting strong management information, if the individual is personally motivated to improve, then this yields the best results.

Therefore, if you can start with personal effectiveness training and then move to project and programme analysis, you are aligning the individual's objectives with that of the business.

2. Employ a 'chaser'
As part of the project and programme support office, define one of the responsibilities of the team as timesheet chaser. They are there to ensure that, each week, timesheets are returned promptly and correctly. Teach that individual negotiation techniques such as, when telephoning a person to follow up their timesheets, use the higher authority technique of:

It's not me, it's the project director who wants them in. When will I get them?

Get the chaser to keep a written log of the excuses that are given. Make it clear, as the manager or director, that you will be actively reviewing the excuses log.

3. Expenses motivator
In designing the timesheet and expense capture system, ensure that any expense claims are checked against the expenses input into the system. The expense claim form will need to be consistent with the coding structure on the expense system. For

---
* Butterworth Heinemann

example, put in date, project code, and split out mileage, subsistence, rail fares, taxi fares and so forth.

If the expense form does not match with the expenses input against the project (by that person), return the form to the employee. This can have a much more immediate effect than the salary motivator.

4. Peer pressure
This is a type of financial motivator. Design a bonus scheme to reward the team as the project or programme progresses. Clearly you need to track deliverables, and one of the ways is through the submission of timesheets. If a member of the team is not performing, and it impacts on the whole team, then there will be peer pressure.

This is a difficult one to play. A balance needs to be struck between peer pressure, which induces a result, and in-fighting, which is destructive.

5. Salary
Within a consultancy business, the consultant can be rewarded based on a chargeable days' bonus. In designing a scheme, link the bonus payments to the invoices raised. Design your system so that invoices are only produced when valid timesheets are submitted. If the timesheet is invalid, this delays the invoice production, which likewise delays the payment of the bonus.

A second idea is to pay a bonus on timesheet entry. For example, if timesheets and expenses are entered in by close of business on a Tuesday for the previous week, for each week in a month, then at month-end a bonus is paid to the employee.

Excuses, comments and other timesheet issues
Below are some comments which I have received in the past, or heard from colleagues, together with suggestions on how to counter them.

You may not believe some of them, but they have been tried. I must admit to thinking that some people are suffering from a severe case of 'excusitis' – inflammation of the excuse-making gland.

What is the mileage to the customer's site?
Excuse: I cannot return my timesheet, as I am unsure of the mileage to the site. My expense claims need to match the timesheet but, without the correct mileage, this is not possible.
Counter: When setting up a project, use a copy of Autoroute to calculate the mileage from your nearest office to the customer's site. Advise the team of this as part of the project initiation process.

I couldn't find a postbox
Excuse: I would post my timesheets to you but there isn't a postbox nearby. (This is primarily where the person keeps manual timesheets.)
Counter: Use a Web-based time-recording program and get the employees to dial in each evening to create their timesheets.

There was no one to sign the timesheets
Excuse: When I left there was no one around so I did not fill in a timesheet. (This is primarily where the person keeps manual timesheets, at the end of the visit getting the customer to sign off the work.)
Counter: Fill in the timesheet anyway. If necessary we can send it to the customer after the event.

I worked late
Excuse: I worked late and did not finish until 11:00 pm. Is this more than 1 day's work? I did not know, so did not return the timesheet.
Counter: Make it clear in the 'Terms and conditions of contract' with the customer what a working day is, eg, 8 hours plus or minus 1 hour. If it is over 9 hours then charge for a part-day thereof. Perhaps put in that evening work is charged at 1.5 times normal day rate. To motivate the employee, you may want to offer overtime payments.

I arrived late but worked late
Excuse: This is a variation on 'I worked late' above. The excuse is that they would not sign it as they were late arriving although they worked into the evening.
Counter: If you are charging for your time, in many organisations they will see what time you arrive but not be there when you leave the site. Of course, the concern is that you are not putting in a full day's work and still charging for the time. Buy the consultant an alarm clock. Arrival times are very important to some people and being late is seen as rudeness.

We achieved very little and I did not know what to write
Excuse: The customer was very talkative and we seemed to achieve very little. So I did not know what to write on the timesheet.
Counter: This can be a thorny problem, especially in a consulting business. You are working with a customer who takes verbosity to new heights. Perhaps they feel the need to talk through the issue to get to a conclusion.

This is managed as follows.

a) Prepare a plan of work for the day and agree this at the outset. As the day progresses, refer to the plan for the day.
b) At the end of the day, do not be rude, but use non-confrontational language to show that the person talked a great deal. For example, 'Extensive discussion took place on this point which delayed the work planned'.

Where there are a number of timesheets with 'extensive discussion' on it you can point to an issue and raise an issue log to manage the problem. Remember that they are paying you, so if you misjudge the wording this could damage the relationship.

Do I really need to track every activity?
Excuse: I was on site for the day. As long as you know the start and end time, then that is all that counts.

Counter: Clearly if the work was the same (eg, user training), then this is not an issue. However, where the work is divided into two or more different activities (installation and user training) we need to have the distinction. See 'Do I need to track every hour?' below.

I did not have any stamps
Excuse: This was in the days before Web-based timesheet entry. The employee would say that they were ready to be posted but needed to get to a post office to purchase some stamps.
Counter: Give them Freepost envelopes. It is preferable to get first-class pre-paid, otherwise there will be the 'it must be delayed in the post' excuse.

Do I need to track every hour?
Excuse: I may do six different things in a day. Do I need to track every hour?
Counter: For those of you who use a Daytimer you will have a sheet which says 'How much is your time worth?' If you are charging for your time then it will be very valuable. Charging £750 per day for a 7.5-hour day is £100 per hour. The numbers are material. If you are paid £40,000 per annum (plus 50% overhead for NI, benefits, office costs, etc), based on 200 productive days (see above on how this figure was derived) then you are costing:

£40,000 + 50% = £60,000
£60,000/200 = £300 per day
£300/7.5 hours in a day = £40 per hour.

For each hour that is not tracked, suggest to the person they take £40 from their wallet and throw it into the bin.

I could not do my timesheets, as I was preparing my expenses
Excuse: I only have so much time, and needed to get my expenses in.
Counter: Make sure that the expenses claims match those on the timesheets. Tell the employee that the first check is consistency with timesheets. Where there is a mismatch, the expense payment will be held up as the detail is examined. This will also act as a basic audit check that what is being claimed is correctly recorded. Where the expenses are recoverable, you are not under-recovering.

I was too busy
Excuse: I was too busy, too tired, not able to, or some other lame excuse.
Counter: This is a pathetic excuse and is coming from a resistor to change.
The people who are resistors to change fall into 3 categories:

- silent
- vocal
- malicious/deliberately stopping.

This is an issue addressed by Stephen Covey in *Principle Centered Leadership*[*].

[*] ISBN 068485841X

Sometimes you have to sidestep people who are negative. Initially, do not confront them, as your positive approach may be causing the problem. Try using peer pressure. If you employ a person as time-recording administrator, who has a responsibility for ensuring timesheets are in, get them to call the individual. Train the administrator in the negotiation technique of higher authority. They can use words like: 'It's not me, it's the project director who is so difficult. Can you help me?'

If the employee persistently disregards the administrator, then you have a disciplinary issue to deal with. Speak to the employee and make it clear that this is a direct instruction. Ask them the question:

Specifically, what prevented you?

List the points one by one that they state and agree a set of actions to overcome these. Do not ask:

Why have you not entered your timesheets?

This will open up a long, rambling monologue.

Without good reason for not completing timesheets, employees are disobeying a direct instruction, which is a disciplinary offence.

Be warned that you cannot accept non-performance in this area. Otherwise the system will fall into disrepute.

I have published the timesheet data and received negative feedback

Excuse: I am reluctant to enter in my timesheets, as the data will not appear to be very good. Alternatively, you may receive fierce feedback when you publish the information.

Counter: When the information is first published, you will probably get a four-stage reaction as below. This is especially the case where the results are not as a person expects.

Denial: There is a period of denial when there are claims that the information is false.

Anger: The person may feel that they have been trapped into reporting what they are doing but not had the opportunity to explain the data.

Rejection: The person may be dispirited and reject the company.

Acceptance: This is the final stage where there is acceptance of the information.

At the acceptance stage, you need to introduce lessons learned and seek to feed the results back into the project or programme life cycle. Some of the lessons will not be seen until the next project or programme. This will make it harder to bring the lessons learned into the organisation, as people forget over time.

Why don't they use a stopwatch function?

This statement may come from your senior management. Record every 15 minutes through the clicking on and off of the stopwatch. The stopwatch function is available in some timesheet programs.

Counter: This is extremely time consuming. More time will be wasted starting and stopping than be effectively recorded.

Where do I post time that is additional work?

Excuse: I cannot post my timesheet, as it is additional work. There is no project or activity created.

Counter: On every project, put in an activity that is for additional time. The analysis of this along with issue logs and contract change notes (CCNs) can give you valuable information about why there are overruns.

If you do not track this, then you could be losing time that is rightly chargeable, or miss an opportunity to learn about common problems that can be rectified through specific management action.

If there is no productive time, there is no reason for the person

There is a company in Sussex, a large organisation, whose IT department have to cross-charge for their time. In cross-charging other departments, they justify their position.

The reasoning they give to people on completing timesheets is:

1. If you have no time to cross charge then you are not productive.
2. If you are not productive then there is no need for your role.
3. If there is no need for your role, you are redundant.

Explain the value of time

Time is a commodity which cannot be re-created. (For a detailed explanation of this see Peter Drucker's book *The effective executive.*) We have a fixed amount of time every day. It is our choice as to how we spend our time. Once the day has past, it cannot be recovered.

If we can put a value on time it is possible to show what the cost of not doing or doing something is (in purely personal terms as opposed to the impact on the project or programme).

Putting a value on time will require relating it to a known item, eg, salary.

Annual salary	Add 50% for overheads	Total	Divide by 252 working days	Per hour (based on 7.5 hours per day)	Per minute
£20,000	£10,000	£30,000	£119	£16	£0.26
£25,000	£12,500	£37,500	£149	£20	£0.33
£30,000	£15,000	£45,000	£179	£24	£0.40
£35,000	£17,500	£52,500	£208	£28	£0.46
£40,000	£20,000	£60,000	£238	£32	£0.53
£45,000	£22,500	£67,500	£268	£36	£0.60
£50,000	£25,000	£75,000	£298	£40	£0.66
£60,000	£30,000	£90,000	£357	£48	£0.79
£70,000	£35,000	£105,000	£417	£56	£0.93

What is the point of performing the work if you are not going to get paid for it?

Time Recording

Invalid time appearing on your project

You need to be careful that time does not get posted to your project that belongs to someone else. In many systems it is possible to set up a list of valid users who can post time to your project.

Recording every 15 minutes of work

I visited a company who were instituting a policy of keeping timesheets for every member of staff. Time was to be kept in 15-minute intervals to enable the tracking of the actual work performed. The finance director commented to me that he thought he would need to set up the following dummy projects:

- Internet surfing
- eating breakfast (their office hours were from 8:00 am)
- office discussion with fellow employees.

After two months of running the system, the employees would realise that, in fact, they did not work as hard as they thought they did!

Closing projects

When the project is completed, remember to close the project to new timesheet entry. There is a danger that employees will post time to an 'old' project. This may be because:

1. There are problems which arose (from the project) that they wanted to hide the time for although the project was closed
2. They have chosen the wrong project when entering timesheets.

Part of the project closure process needs to include updating the time-recording system to include this.

Ways to avoid accountability

The 'Resource planning and utilisation' chapter gives a proposed budgeting model for employee utilisation. Once every hour of the day is being tracked, then an employee must be accountable for their actions. The sorts of arguments which are given (I think) to avoid accountability are:

Excuse: I am a chargeable resource, so it is my chargeable time which is important. I will only record revenue earning days.
Counter: All time is important, what other work is more important than earning revenue?

Excuse: I am a pre-sales resource, so there is no point is recording my time.
Counter: It is important to track the time required to bid for business, and the end-to-end time from initial contact to project signing. Detailed time analysis gives us this information.

Excuse: The time-recording system is not helpful in getting timesheets out in an analysable format.
Counter: Change the time-recording system to one which enables data to be analysed quickly and easily. In the meantime, get an admin person to extract data and get some high-level numbers.

Excuse: I am too busy to enter in timesheets weekly, so will put them in monthly.
Counter: A month is too long. After one month, things can change, so get them entered in weekly.

Excuse: There is no work. For example, in a professional services business, the consultant says that, as there is no booking in their diary, they stayed at home.
Counter: Set up a project called 'No booking'. If there is extensive evidence of this, then you are over-resourced.

Remember that data that is not available cannot be analysed! I suggest that data that is not available is described as time wasting.

Conclusion

Timesheets and time analysis allow you to:

- understand how effective your estimating is
- understand what individuals are doing in the team
- identify common problems and therefore focus management effort on improvement programmes
- Calculate utilisation and effectiveness of resource planning.

Do not underestimate the work involved in getting timesheets returned correctly completed. Persistent vigilance is needed.

The individual may believe that once the data is collected, there is no further action. With data in the time-recording system, the analysis can begin. This is where the real work starts – making sense of the data and doing something with it.

'But what work – operational improvements, strategic changes?' you may be saying to yourself. In the chapter on reporting (page 123) there is a list of questions that are worth considering as a starting point to this analysis.

EXPENSES

Introduction

This chapter looks at the issue of expenses, typically out-of-pocket expenses incurred by people working on a programme or project.

Expenses on a programme or project that covers multiple sites will represent a significant cost. Even travelling to a single site, there will be an overhead incurred by subcontracting staff. At the start of the project or programme, a budgeted cost for expenses will need to be identified.

In any organisation there should be guidelines for what is recognised as a legitimate expense. A dispensation from the Inland Revenue will assist in filling in the personal tax return at the end of the year.

Where to capture?

The expenses should be captured through the time-recording system. In the chapter on time recording, the matching of expense claims with timesheet entries was identified as a mechanism for ensuring timesheets were completed. This should have the added benefit of guaranteeing that expenses are entered promptly.

Expense analysis

At the end of the project or programme, expense analysis should take place. In the nominal ledger it is likely that expense recovery is shown as a total amount with no breakdown. What is of interest is the analysis of expenses by type of expense.

In capturing expenses, the system should be able to store, for example:

- petrol/mileage
- taxis
- rail & underground
- parking
- subsistence (where there is no hotel cost)
- hotel accommodation
- entertaining
- other.

There is a saying that the role of the project manager is to 'buy the beer'. To motivate the team will require much entertaining. It is difficult to recover this cost from the client. (Also, buying them dinner and then charging them for it is not seen as good form.)

For each of the above, it should be possible to see the level of recovery; so that in the internal project closure and 'lessons learned', the efficacy of the project or programme accounting function can include expense cost and expense recovery analysis.

Expenses and IT services businesses

For organisations that charge for their services, there is the option of trying to recover expenses through re-charging the customer.

To understand the potential impact of expenses on profitability, let's look at an example:

- We are charging £850 per day for consultancy
- No expenses are to be recovered
- Our net profit as a business is 10%, £85
- Each consultancy visit incurs £20 in expenses.

What is our expense cost?

- Is it £20/£850 = 2.35%
- or £20/£85 = 23.53%?

On 10% net profit before tax as a business, one day of consultancy should achieve £85 net profit. So, the £20 expenses represent a 23.53% reduction in our net profit. This is much more significant and should therefore guide our thinking.

Recovering expense costs

At this point, you want to identify the alternative approaches looking at what could be recovered from the customer. There are a number of approaches to consider.

1. Recover at cost
2. Recover with a mark-up
3. Absorb the cost
4. Partial recovery
5. Use their rates.

For all the options (except number 3), you must get the expenses entered at the same time as the timesheets.

Recover at cost

Here the amount claimed by a person is the amount invoiced to a customer.

Advantages
- It is a straightforward re-charge of what is put in the time-recording and expense system. Little administrative overhead is required as the invoices raised are based on the amounts entered by the individual.
- If there is negotiation with the customer over the price of the contract, offering recovery at cost or no recovery shows flexibility.

Disadvantages
- Employees may claim different amounts depending on where they travel from (different places of work). The customer can query these.
- Petrol costs represent only a portion of the costs of running a vehicle. Organisations such as the Automobile Association publish mileage rates which include insurance, depreciation, servicing, road tax and all the other costs. So, if you re-charge the customer based only on a petrol mileage rate, then you may be missing out.

Recover with a mark-up

If mileage rates do not represent the true cost of running a vehicle, then why not mark up the amount claimed to represent a more realistic figure? This is what is achieved with a mark-up. For each mile that is claimed, recharge at an approved rate (such as the Automobile Association one).

Advantages
- The project profitability is improved, as there is significantly better recovery than that with a recovery at cost.

Disadvantages
- In quoting for work, the customer may look at expenses as part of the project cost and calculate what could be claimed. On an £850 per day charge with a round trip of 60 miles at 40p per mile, the mileage claim would be £24 (40p x 60 miles.) This is an additional 2.82% on the cost of a consultancy day.
- There is an administrative overhead. The time and expense recording system will hold the amount claimed but might not hold the number of miles. (For P11D purpose these only need to be calculated at year-end.) It is now necessary to hold the return mileage from your offices to the customer and then for each expense claim where there is a petrol entry, re-charge based on an algorithm.

Absorb the cost

Here you do not attempt to recharge the expenses but simply absorb the cost. The amount claimed is included as part of the daily rate. (You may need to increase the day rate.)

Advantages
- It is straightforward. There is no recovery.
- It could be presented to the customer as a reduction in the price of consultancy. (Although I doubt whether this would be believed!)

Disadvantages
- Expenses are being incurred which come straight off the profit line. The impact of this was detailed in the introduction to this section and its importance cannot be over-emphasised.
- At project budgeting, it will be necessary to identify expenses as a cost and then track actual versus budget. With a recovery option, expenses are not an issue.
- Using the example above of a day rate of £850, this could rise to £874 (at £24 cost). This could appear as pricing you out of the consultancy market, as your rates have gone up. In addition, there is still the reporting of expenses incurred in the profit and loss account, and the fact that part of the consultancy rate includes expenses is likely to be forgotten.
- If the budgeting for expenses at the start of the project or programme is too low, then any additional expense cost over budget will reduce the expected profit.

Partial recovery
Here you do not attempt to recharge the expenses as claimed or based on a mark-up. The recovery is a flat fee. Agree with the client that for each site visit there is a flat charge per day.

Advantages
- It is straightforward. There is a flat fee per day on site charged to the client.
- The expected amount to be received can be calculated at the start of the project.
- If a charge of £20 per visit can be included in the contract for work that is inside a given geographical area (such as the M25), then this is a non-contentious value. On our 141 days of revenue-earning work (see the 'Utilisation in a consulting business' section of the 'Resource planning and utilisation' examples), it will net £2,820 in income. Multiply this by the number in your team, and the totals will soon become significant.

Disadvantages
- How to agree a fair amount? During contract negotiation it is an item which is to be resolved. The customer may want to use it as a bargaining tool. This is a conversation that you may not wish to have.
- Does the time and expense recording system allow for this functionality? If not then it is a non-runner anyway.

Use their rates
This may be the easiest to negotiate. On the basis that you are asking for reimbursement in a manner which is consistent with their team, this is fair for both parties. The amount claimed could be a combination of partial recovery and mark-up.

Advantages
- It can be easier to negotiate and may prove to be more generous than you would normally offer.
- It is harder during negotiation stage for the customer to refute this approach.

Disadvantages
- Some organisations have very complex expense-claim systems; eg, different mileage rates based on miles per annum, overnight allowances, overseas allowances and so forth. The administrative overhead could be significant.
- It is another thing to understand during the project or programme. Complexity is exponential and do you really want to have to think in terms of their expense claim process on top of all the project issues?
- Likewise, the amount claimed could be inconsistent with your Inland Revenue dispensation as an organisation. This brings an overhead for all self-assessment individuals and your finance department when it comes to P11D time.

Conclusion
If expense analysis has not been performed in the past, then budgeting this by project or programme is finger in the air work. (The financial accounts will contain totals by

employee by cost centre, not likely to be analysed further.) In the contract negotiation stage, expense recovery is not normally an item to be discussed, let alone negotiated.

Many consulting firms charge expenses unless it is a fare on the Underground or an amount that is equally immaterial. Expense analysis is also covered in the reporting chapter.

A closing thought: be careful when recharging expenses that you do not recharge entertaining. The client will not appreciate receiving an invoice for that fine meal which you said was your company's thank you for their business!

Section Two: Advanced concepts

This section builds on the concepts covered in Section One by considering:

- Advanced design concepts
- Change control
- Contract terms
- Resource planning examples.

ADVANCED DESIGN CONCEPTS
Complex relationships

The aim is to design a system that will give cross-project and programme analysis.

Consider that you are running a business of 2,000 consultants working across multiple sites, both local and foreign. There will be multiple customers and multiple programmes. Indeed, a single customer might be running a programme and a number of separate projects with your business (the single customer being a multinational organisation).

To obtain information about these multiple projects and programmes, you need to create a hierarchy which will take these factors into consideration. (See diagram overleaf.)

This is the first view of a complex relationship. Here you have a customer who has one or more programmes under way. The programmes themselves have customers. Each customer has one or more projects.

For example: an international hotel group (Customer 1) has a programme to standardise their internal systems. This involves everything from the type of mini-bar, door locks, and check-in room software to the accounting system at the back office. They contract with a number of suppliers who each run a programme of projects. So, a project could be to implement a new financial accounting system at a hotel.

The hotel group may not own the properties but have management contracts. The contract for the supply is with the owning companies of the individual hotels (Customer 2), not the international hotel group. The paying customer is a different legal entity from the initiator of the programme.

The customer at 1 is not necessarily the same as the customer at 2. Our Customer 2 may have multiple hotels, which are each then a project in their own right.

Customer 2 is likely to be the debtor in the sales ledger. Customer 1 is the pre-sales contact. Within the project repository, there needs to be a mechanism to link these two.

Question: Can you identify and report this from your current system?

Project and Programme Accounting

One customer has one or more Programmes
The Programme has one or more Customers

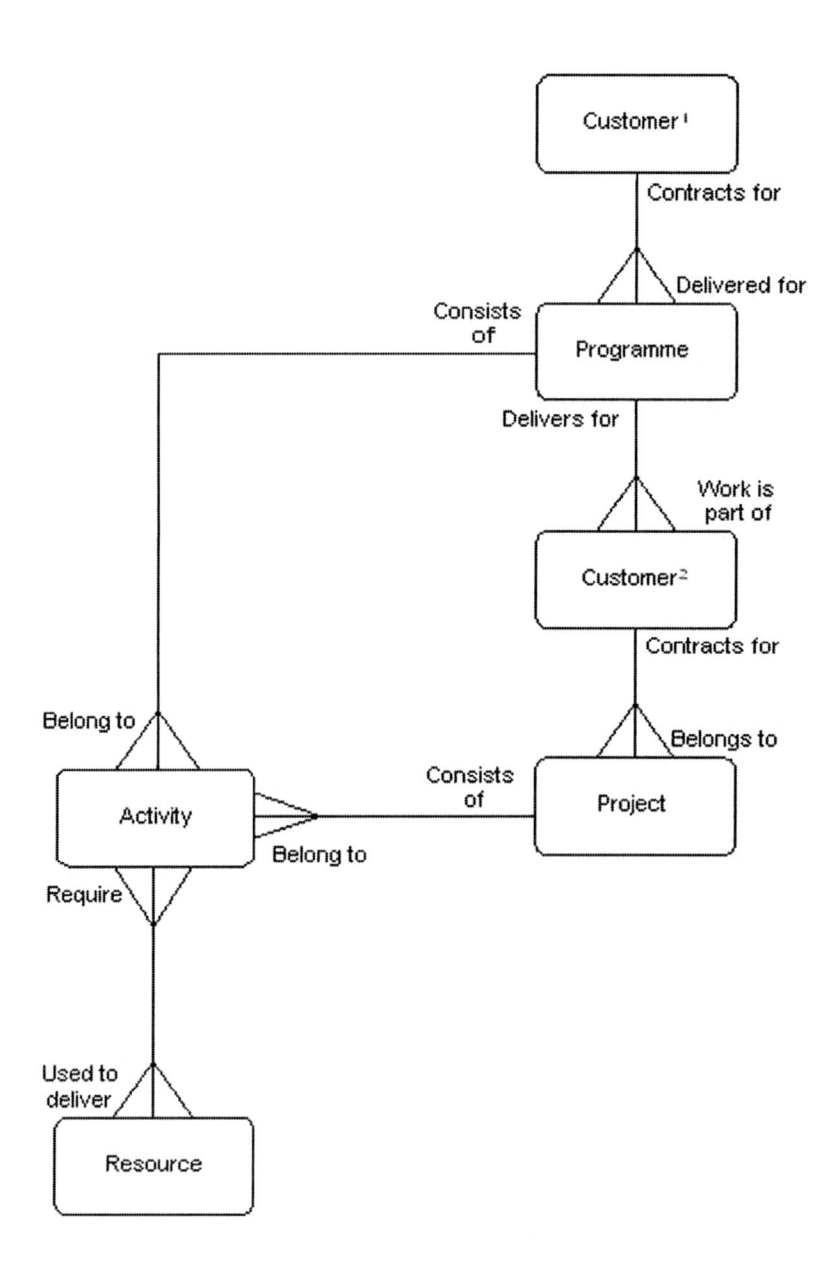

- Customer[1]
  - Contracts for / Delivered for
- Programme
  - Consists of (to Activity)
  - Delivers for / Work is part of
- Customer[2]
  - Contracts for / Belongs to
- Project
  - Consists of (to Activity) / Belong to
- Activity
  - Belong to (to Programme)
  - Require / Used to deliver
- Resource

92

Advanced Design Concepts

Now we put a programme at the top of the hierarchy. So, the second diagram is an extension of that presented earlier.

Combining them together

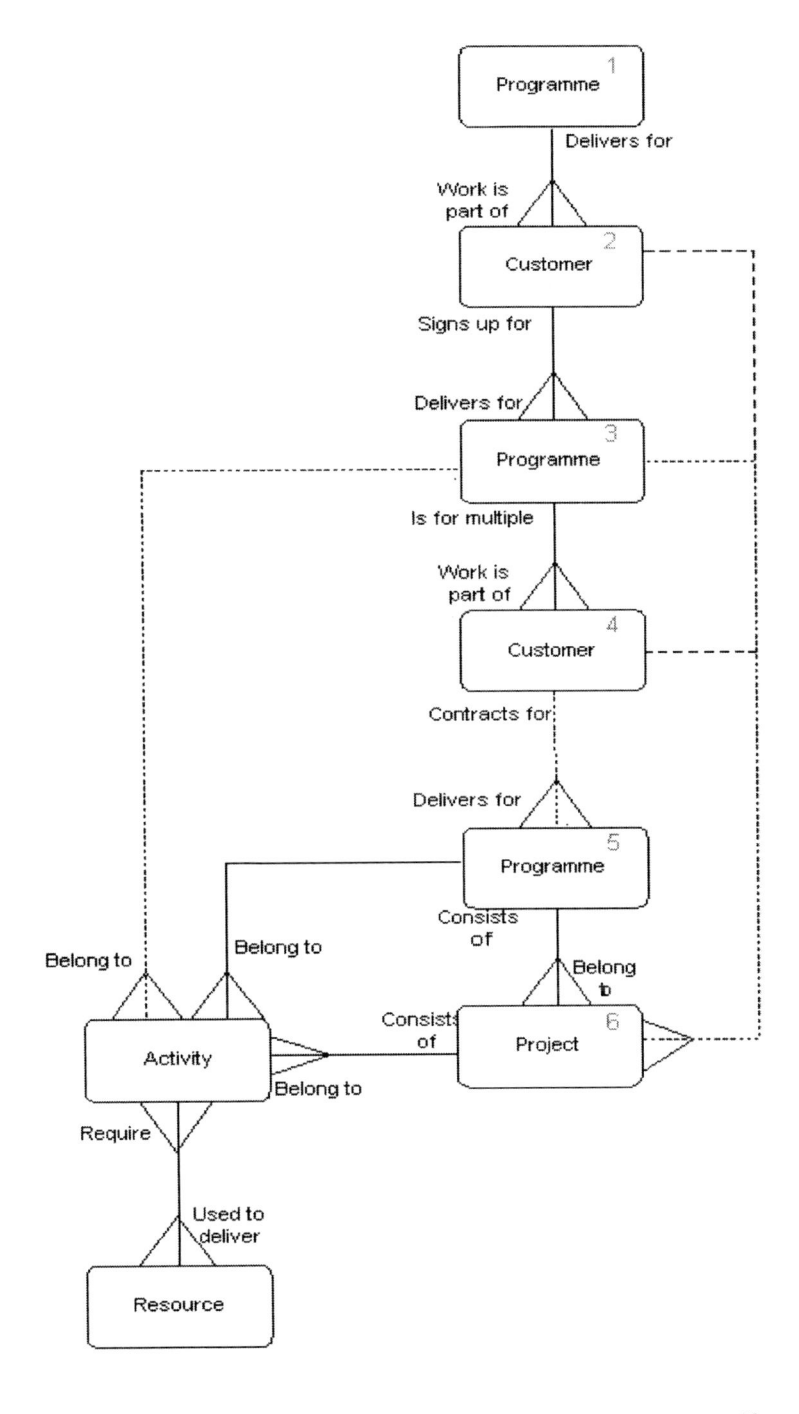

I have numbered the entities to assist in understanding the structure.

The customer at 1 is not necessarily the same as the customer at 2. Our Customer 2 may have multiple hotels, which are each, then a project in their own right.

Customer 2 is likely to be the debtor in the sales ledger. Customer 1 is the pre-sales contact. Within the project repository, there needs to be a mechanism to link these two.

Question: Can you identify and report this from your current system?

Now we put a programme at the top of the hierarchy. So the following diagram is an extension of that presented earlier.

I have numbered the entities to assist in understanding the structure.

Examples of the above

Example 1

A systems solution company has a programme under way to implement financial accounting systems (this implementation programme consists of repeater projects). The implementation programme has its generic characteristics (standard of delivery, competencies of personnel, version of accounting system to be implemented, and so forth). There are multiple customers who sign up to this programme. Each customer will have one or more projects under way (entities 1, 2 and 6).

Example 2

A systems solution company has a programme under way to implement financial accounting systems (the implementation programme: entity 1).

The implementation programme has its generic characteristics (standard of delivery, competencies of personnel, version of accounting system to be implemented, and so forth).

An international hotel group (entity 2) decides to run a programme of implementing new accounting systems (entity 3) with a particular company. The company who are awarded this contract then have the programme of projects.

This programme has one or more customers (entity 4) who may have one or more projects (entity 6). The hotel group may not own the properties but have management contracts. The contract for the supply is with the owning companies of the individual hotels, not the international hotel group. The paying customer is a different legal entity from the initiator of the programme.

However, the customer could have a programme (entity 5) for themselves, as there are multiple projects across multiple sites. The activities and resources can be applied to the projects and programmes.

Question: Can you identify this from your system?

Is this not possible through the accounting system?

Many accounting systems store data by customer with some level of project analysis. The difficulty here is that there are two separate customers, and three separate programmes.

The invoicing will be to a specific customer, and without a flag, analysis code or some other link between customer set-up and the project set-up, the drawing together of this information will not be easy, or even possible, to perform.

Advanced Design Concepts

Beyond projects and programmes to employees
The employee perspective

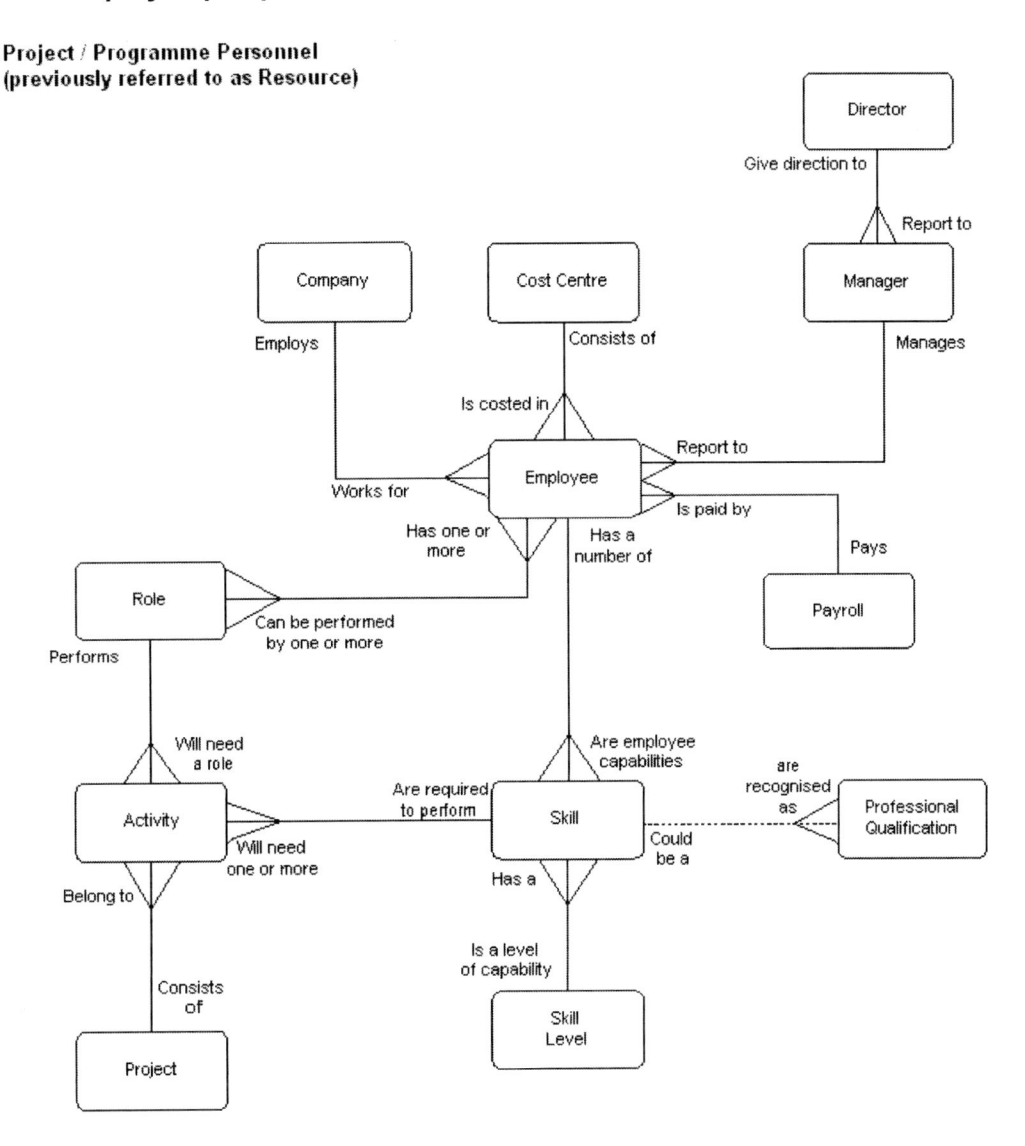

Project / Programme Personnel
(previously referred to as Resource)

By extending the design through to the personnel working on the project or programme, we are able to bring a holistic view to the approach.

At the centre we have the employee (resource). On the previous diagrams the activity was linked directly to the resource (employee in this case.) I have expanded this for completeness.

Entity (related to employee)	Reason for relationship
Cost centre	An employee is in a cost centre. This could to link back to the financial accounts.
Company	An employee works for a company. If the organisation uses subcontractors then you need to distinguish whom the person works for. Subcontractors are unlikely to be paid through the payroll but would be located in a cost centre.
Manager	An employee has a manager. You may have people allocated to your project or programme, but if there are employee issues you need to refer to the manager. Analysis of the work performed by a manager's team could be important for the director.
Director	A manager has a director. In deeply hierarchical organisations then this would be more complex.
Skill	The employee has one or more skills. The skills are a combination of activities they can perform (which might be types of consulting service for a chargeable business), professional qualifications and levels of ability. In showing this it is recognising that, by designing the employee appraisal and development process in line with the activities of the company, there is a strategic fit between what the employee wants to achieve and the company's needs to reach its strategic goals.
Skill level	Understanding the level of skill could be used to look at productivity levels. In cost estimation there is a method of looking at team performance codes. When quoting for a project or programme, the quote is based on a person delivering one day of work. Recognising that some people are more productive than others, this is to enable the project or programme manager to understand a person's productivity relative to the standard.
Professional qualifications	This is important in cases where specific industry skills are required.
Role	An employee has one or more roles. There are a number of roles on a project or programme. One or more people may perform each role (eg, trainer).
Activity	The activities in a service-based business are called service. If our employee has skills based on software modules and services, and these are booked on to projects or programmes which have that specific need, our productivity should be higher, as there is a reduced learning curve. In internal IT departments, the skills might be based on supporting the existing infrastructure, running new projects or like items.
Project	This is shown for completeness to link back to the other diagrams.

Advanced Design Concepts

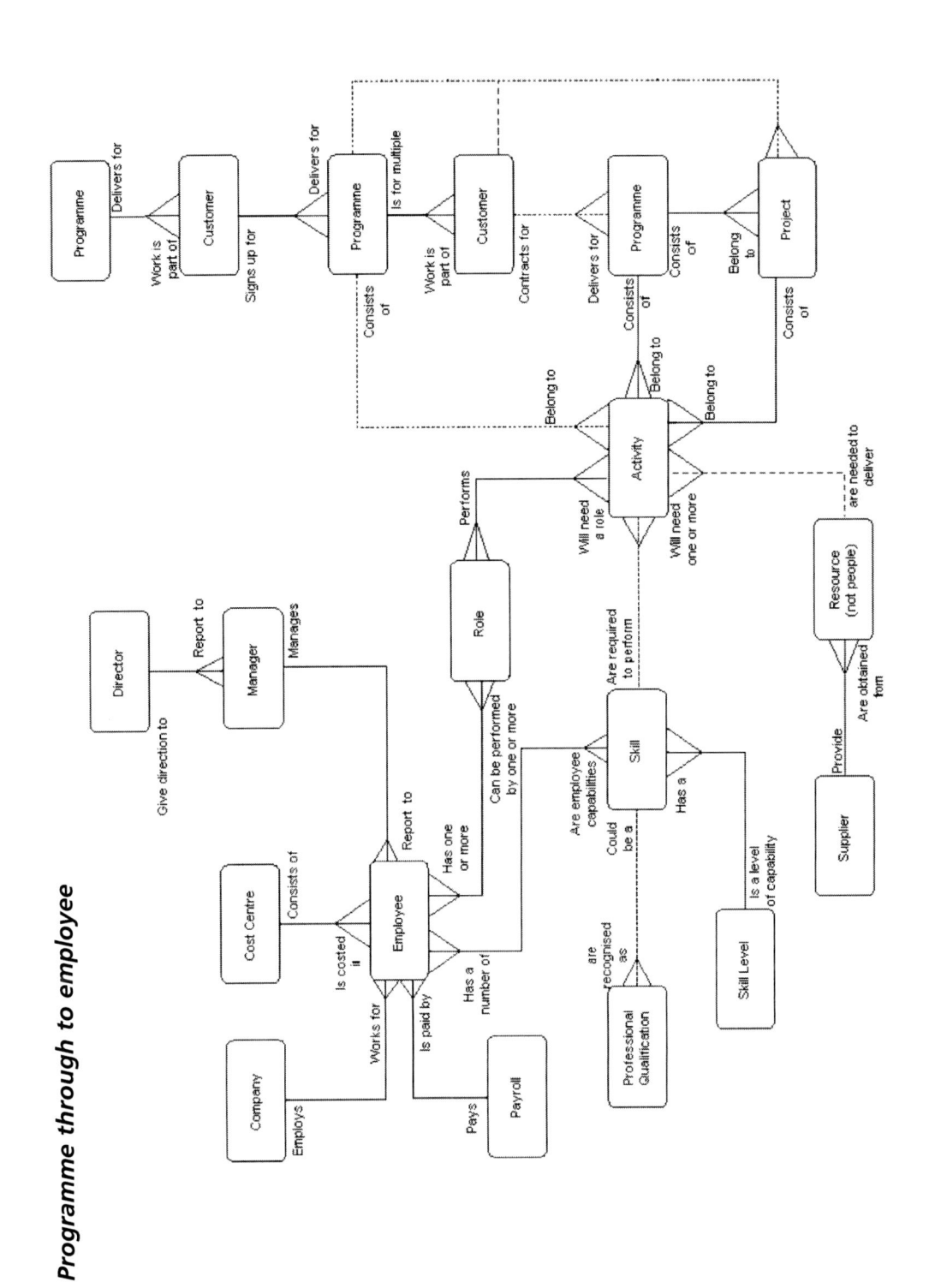

Programme through to employee

Project and Programme Accounting

In bringing the programme model together with the employee model we can see the scope and complexity of the relationships. The resource (not people) entity is separated out whereas previously it was one composite entity.

Question:
a) Can you draw this type of relationship for your business?
b) How does your company align the development of skills with the services offered?

Example structures
Two example structures are given:

- the training company example
- the help-desk example.

The training company example
Assume that you are running a training company. In this instance, you want to store details on the activities being performed:

a) by the area of learning
b) by a subject (which is grouped into areas)
c) by the trainer – to get some utilisation analysis.

The representation of the relationships could be:

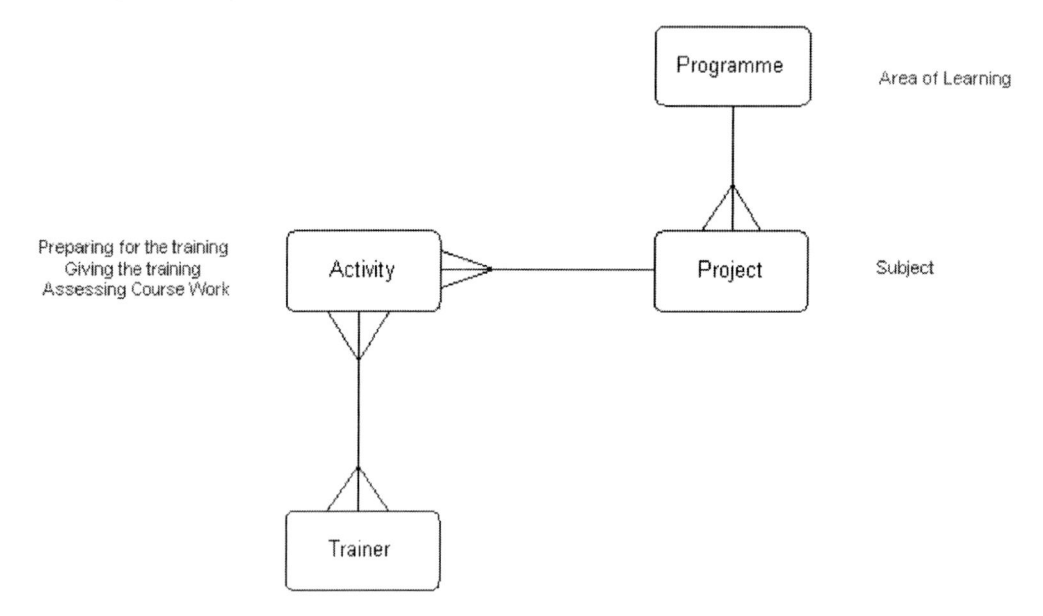

```
                                              ┌───────────┐
                                              │ Programme │    Area of Learning
                                              └─────┬─────┘
                                                    │
                                                   /│\
                                                    │
Preparing for the training   ┌──────────┐     ┌─────┴─────┐
   Giving the training       │ Activity ├────<│  Project  │    Subject
 Assessing Course Work        └────┬─────┘     └───────────┘
                                   │
                                  /│\
                                   │
                              ┌────┴────┐
                              │ Trainer │
                              └─────────┘
```

Projects are created under a programme – which is used to group projects together. The programme could be a subject area, an area of learning, or perhaps all the projects under one director.

Activities are created for a project to cover the main work performed, such as:

98

- training course preparation
- running a training course
- write up assessment of the course
- visiting trainees who are at work (for work appraisal).

The trainer enters time against the activity.

As well as the above, time would also be entered for the 'dummy projects' of holiday, training, absence, etc, to ensure that the total utilisation can be analysed.

The help desk example

Assume that you are running a telephone help desk. You provide telephone assistance either to external customers or you are an internal IT department.

The representation of the relationships could be:

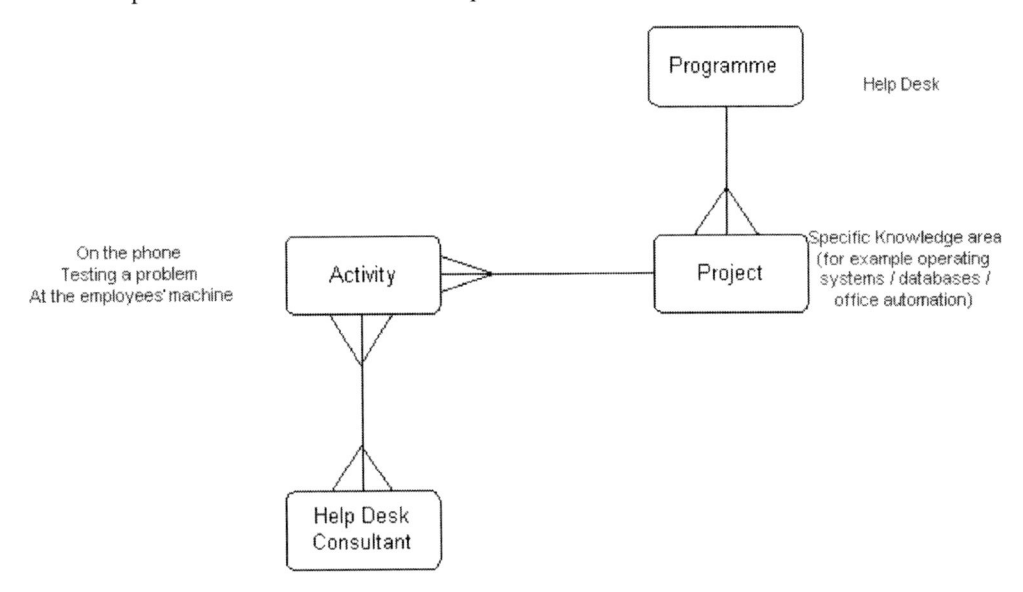

```
                              Programme
                                  |                Help Desk
                                  |
                                  △
                                 ╱ ╲
                                ╱   ╲
 On the phone                  ╱     ╲       Specific Knowledge area
 Testing a problem    Activity ━━━━━ Project  (for example operating
 At the employees' machine                    systems / databases /
                              △                office automation)
                             ╱ ╲
                            ╱   ╲
                         Help Desk
                         Consultant
```

The programme is the provision of help desk services. The projects created under the programme are for each major type of support provided, eg, an operating system support project, a database support project.

Activities are created for a project to cover the main work performed, such as:

- on the phone answering a question
- testing a problem to find a resolution
- working at an employee's machine.

The help desk consultant enters time against the activity. The advantage here is that with a detail of the time spent on support, and the number of calls taken, it is possible to calculate the efficiency and efficacy of an employee.

(As well as the above, they would also enter time for the 'dummy projects' of holiday, training, absence, etc, to ensure that the total utilisation can be analysed.)

Further points to consider
Activities and levels of granularity
When planning the project, the work is divided into activities. In PRINCE2, there is a list of deliverables and each deliverable has one or more activities required to complete the deliverable (the product).

For budgeting purposes, this analysis enables us to identify the total cost and possibly the total revenue.

The trade-off is to give sufficient levels of detail in planning but to ensure that this can be aligned to the capture of the actuals (this is covered in more depth in the chapter on budgeting, page 28). Suffice to say, if the activity-level planning is too detailed, it may not be possible to collect the actual data and the meaning is lost.

There is more information in the chapter on budgeting on activity-level analysis and aligning this to timesheets and project planning.

Inventory and purchases for the project
What happens when stock is required for the project? In designing a solution, it is important that each stock item is tracked on a project-by-project basis; the tracking being from purchase through to use and, where applicable, posting to the fixed asset register.

In the diagram on page 97, the stock item is taken as a resource. There is a more detailed explanation of the resource structure in the budgeting chapter.

Suffice to say, the classification of resources needs to be grouped together, and in reviewing the requirements for your own system, identify if a stock item purchase could be grouped together for reporting and analysis purposes.

End-to-end analysis
Projects and programmes are about the delivery of a solution and/or changing the organisation. At the end of the project or programme, the team are disbanded and business-as-usual proceeds.

In designing the solution, if you consider that there is a life cycle to purchases (such as inventory items which are used by the business), then how can the costs be tracked for those subsequent purchases? This requires the review of the maintenance system and checking that line item analysis is possible.

User locations
When designing the solution, it is important to remember the location of users. Internal departments who service users who are on the local area network will not have the same constraints as organisations who work across multiple sites. For example, see the diagram opposite.

Advanced Design Concepts

Programme and Project Accounting Example User Map

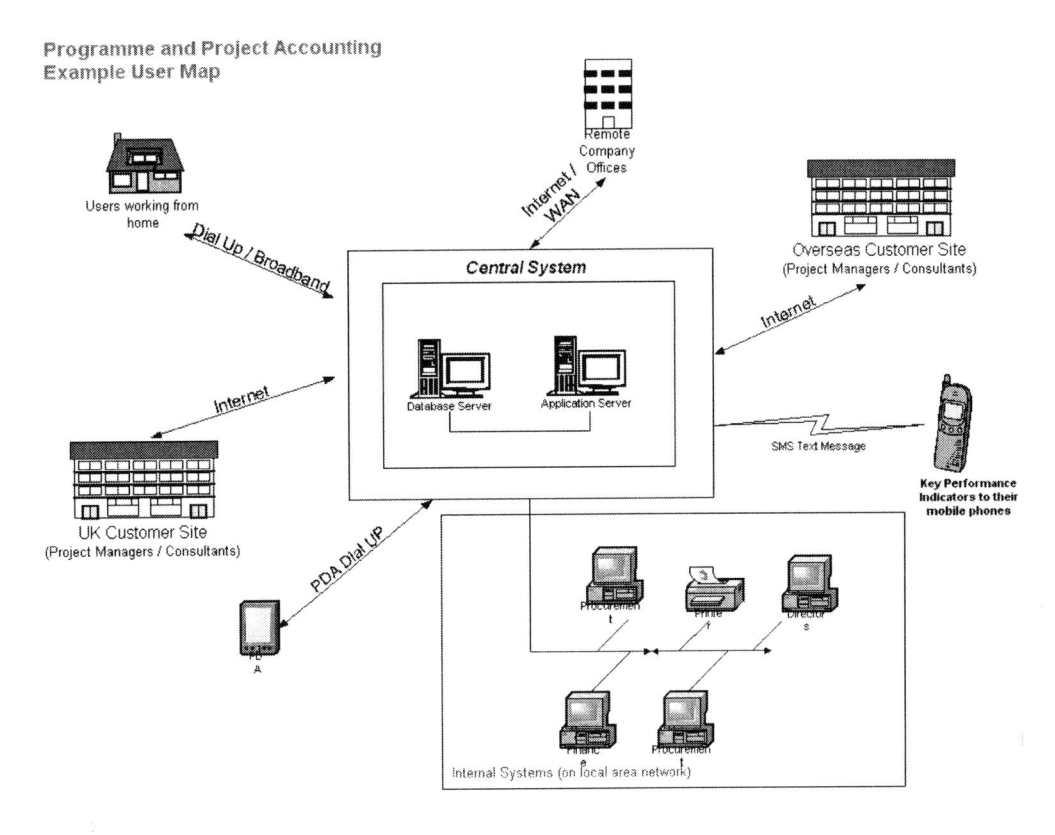

Remote workers still need the functionality of entry of data, reporting information and obtaining feedback quickly and easily. When implementing a project accounting solution, we need to identify the separate user locations where access could be required.

Summary
With a clear understanding of the design requirements, the physical implementation of the system will enable the development of a strong coding structure. From this, the data that is entered can be analysed.

CHANGE CONTROL

Introduction

Here is an interesting problem. The purpose of the change control note (CCN) is to record changes to the project or programme in the areas of:

- revenue
- cost
- time or timescales
- quality.

Within the project or programme accounting area, you need to track the changes to cost or time. How can these be represented in the project or programme reporting system?

Objectives

Your objectives from an accounting and reporting perspective are to track:

What changes in timescales occur during the project?
The contract will have deadlines against which payments are made. If the timescales change, although the overall cost or revenue may not, this could impact on your payment dates. Cash is king and without payment you could suffer through additional interest charges on the business, or worst still, run out of cash.

What changes are occurring in cost?
Identifying changes in cost can assist in highlighting problems with your programme or project techniques. For example, what if your company is persistently under-quoting for projects? The analysis of change control could highlight this, and give justification for a reworking of processes.

What increased revenue comes through change control?
An ordinary debtors' ledger and customer analysis will show the revenue for a customer and, through your project reporting, the revenue by project. What you need to understand are the changes in revenue arising from change control.

Revenue

There is an opportunity to increase the revenue from the programme through the use of change control. Recognising revenue opportunities and taking advantage of these can bring additional reward without the same level of pre-sales activity required to win the original business.

A fine line must be drawn between presenting more opportunity and the customer seeing you as an avaricious organisation!

Cost

Naturally it is your aim to limit cost unless there is a corresponding increase in revenue.

However, there are occasions when the costs will increase and there is no revenue to match it. In the budgeting chapter, you saw that the tracking of actuals is very difficult. Therefore, it is important that changes to cost budgets are recorded, together with their reasons.

I suggest that you identify where additional costs can come from in your line of business, and how you can trap them. From this, a management action plan can be developed to put in preventative measures.

Likewise, do not forget that a project or programme can be de-scoped. This will reduce cost but also may reduce revenue.

The challenge

Do you view a CCN as a new project in the programme, or a change to the existing project? Why the distinction? The answer may be due to the way your system works, although the distinction should be looked at as:

1. If there is a change to the project revenue, then the revenue budget will need to be amended.
2. If there is a change to the project cost, then the cost budget will need to be amended.
3. If there is a change to the project timescales, then the project revenue and cash-flow forecasts may need to be amended.

The questions to ask:
1. How to change budgets and track the change?
2. Is the CCN significant (in financial terms) and therefore warrants tracking as a separate project?
3. Is the CCN to extend an existing activity only?

New project or programme or budget change

The initial driver is to capture the change in the project or programme. You can create a new project in the programme to hold this budget information.

When to create a new project in the programme

Assuming that the work is easily identified – such as a new deliverable – then a new project could be created in the programme. The source of the project is the CCN and within the project analysis categories (which many systems have) it will need flagging that it is through a CCN. This will give you the analysis of work from CCNs.

When to amend the project or programme budget

If you were working on a deliverable and the revenue or costs change (in the costs, I mean the days to be performed which are then translated into costs), then it would be better to uplift (or downgrade) the budget for revenue or cost. In capturing time through a timesheet system, it is difficult enough to get the details entered, but asking someone to separate out the time through a change in budget on a deliverable, I believe, will require more effort than it is worth.

The tracking of change control notes of this type could be performed manually or, using a simple spreadsheet listing, change note number, description, revenue, cost, reason (with some reason code analysis) and date. This should be set up in the project or programme support office to ensure that the view is across the whole project and programmes under the programmes.

What to do with non-time CCNs?
The initial challenge was where to record the change for time entries. Depending on your system, if it is for additional capital expenditure then, unless you have a project accounting module, the change would be recorded in the sales order processing system (where revenue is involved) and, if it is a cost that you incur without recovery, in the purchase order processing system. Whichever way, it is important that the details are recorded, along with the reason why, and can be linked to the project or programme.

> *Hints:* Here are a few hints to keep in mind when preparing a CCN.
> a) Try and identify the sign-off level of the person you are working with. Then prepare CCNs that are within their budget.
> b) Remember to include the time to write the CCN.
> c) Ensure that your team are aware of any revised project codes for their timesheets if they are working on the CCN area.
> d) Make sure that additional revenue/cost items such as expenses are covered within the scope of the CCN. consider employing an administrative assistant. They will be considerably cheaper than employing your highly skilled individuals to do this work.

CONTRACT TERMS
Overview
The ease with which a project or programme turns into revenue and cash is affected by the contract terms which have been negotiated.

Depending on your organisation, there may be specific contract types that are put in place. In software development this could be based around a fixed price, with payment terms based on delivery. For pure consulting, it might be time and materials.

Whichever type is used, the revenue and spend will not be linear, ie, in the review of reports, do not expect that the sales invoices or purchase invoices will match off easily.

Here, we are seeking to improve the position, but accept that it will never be ideal. The four areas to consider are:

- nature of the contract
- terms of delivery
- invoicing
- payment.

The legal issues such as warranty, acceptance, transfer of ownership, are not covered. For more information on this, there are many fine contract books.

Nature of the contract
The contractual terms may be: fixed price, cost plus, time and materials, or a combination of these.

In negotiating the contract with the client and, if necessary, the back-to-back contract with a supplier, the key considerations are invoicing and cash.

Terms of delivery
How the project is delivered will be negotiated, based on the type of work. For example, with a software development project, as programs are written and tested, they would be combined into modular groups. As a group is completed, it could be delivered to the customer.

In PRINCE2, the deliverables are identified in terms of 'Product'. A Product Definition is written, the activities listed, then, when the activities are completed, the Product should have been delivered.

Invoicing
The ideal position is to invoice as soon as possible, to get the revenue on to the profit and loss account. Of course, you need to be aware of the revenue recognition issues. (See the receivables or sales ledger chapter, page 46, for a detailed discussion.)

The methods of invoicing include:

- deposit
- upfront
- as performed.

Deposit

To obtain a deposit payment from a company, it is often necessary to produce some legal document, eg, an invoice. The invoice cannot be put onto the profit and loss account but will be written to work-in-progress.

When reviewing the programme or project reports, look at how the system analyses deposit invoices.

Upfront

In offering an invoice upfront, it may be that you are seeking to reduce the amount of paperwork. Some companies motivate their sales team with commission received when invoices are raised.

The sales incentive is there to get an invoice raised. This type of approach is useful on consultancy contracts where the work is performed on a time and material basis. There are no cash receipt problems and, as time is entered into the time-recording system, the revenue is recognised on to the profit and loss account.

The downside here is that expenses might need to be invoiced separately. Sending invoices for expenses, which can be small amounts, could appear petty.

The project or programme accounting system will need to allow for the production of invoice(s) upfront; perhaps in blocks of days, or for the whole contract.

As performed

The invoicing for work 'as performed' could mean on a time and materials approach, or as a product is delivered ('Product' in the PRINCE2 sense).

There needs to be a mechanism in place, either manual or automatic, to ensure that when an action happens, such as the installation of software, or delivery of a design document, then an invoice is produced.

Payment

Cash is king. For an organisation that is in the revenue-producing business, then the collection of payment is paramount. In reviewing your contract terms, look at the cash payment terms, and then think about ways to get the money sooner from the client, and pay out later to the supplier and/or subcontractor. Of course, the ideal position is to obtain all the money upfront, and then start work!

Conclusion

Look at the terms of contract that are negotiated for your projects and programmes. Identify the improvements that you would like to introduce (such as when invoices can be raised, payments received). These need to be fed back into the sales process and the operational systems set-up to ensure that these can be delivered against.

RESOURCE PLANNING & UTILISATION EXAMPLES
Utilisation in consulting businesses

The previous resource-planning chapter (see page 69) identified 200 productive days. In a consulting organisation, the reality is likely to be less. Some examples and the background reasoning for this are given below.

Pre-sales time

For those of you who are in the consulting services industry, to achieve 200 chargeable days would be tremendous. However, many consultants are used in pre-sales (working with sales to tender for business) as well as a chargeable resource. This sales activity will depress the revenue-earning ability as you make provision for this time.

Unless you have previously collected metrics on what level is required, then the number you choose will be guessed. I would suggest you start at 15% of the total revenue-earning time (200 days.) This is 30 days in total; that averages out at 2.5 days per month.

Why make provision for pre-sales time? In the revenue budgets, if you were not aware of this pre-sales figure then your revenue projections would be 17.6% higher than realistically achievable (200 − 15% (30) = 170. 30/170 = 17.6%). Do you really want to report this to your managing director or financial director?

Hint: When setting up the pre-sales project, it might be better to allocate an amount by sales person or sales team. A central pool of time will get used quicker than if it is perceived to be capped by person.

The Christmas period

Christmas is a difficult time in the consulting business. Clients do not usually want a consultant on site if they are not themselves going to be available. Calculating the impact of Christmas is given below.

Description	Lost days
If Christmas Day is on a Wednesday then it is unlikely you will get any bookings for Monday 23rd, Tuesday 24th, Friday 27th, Monday 30th and Tuesday 31st December.	5
In this example, New Year's day is on a Wednesday, so the 2nd and 3rd January are likely to be non-productive. Who will want bookings on these 2 days?	2
Total Christmas period days	7

Other items to consider are the Christmas party or the summer party where your team will want to be in the office or get away early so they can get ready!

Travel time: UK

In a consultancy service organisation, if you book work on an hourly or part-day basis, then travel time can limit the productive day. For example, your consultant is booked to visit a site for half a day, the customer is in Brighton, and your own offices are in the City of London. Travel time from a half-day morning visit, after lunch, would bring the consultant to your offices mid-afternoon. If they have visited another site, which is unlikely to be local, then they would again arrive mid-afternoon. Not an ideal situation.

There are two issues here. Firstly, the travel time is now during office hours. As a consultant, travel is part of the job but would normally be before 9.00 am and after 5.30 pm. Is the travel time charged to the customer or written off? Secondly, you need to decide how to record this time. If you are charging it to the client, it should be posted as travel time (or perhaps 'call out charge' which is probably more acceptable). If it is not charged to the client you will need to set up a project to which to post this time.

In the second instance, this will give you an indication to the materiality of the time lost through travel.

But how many days should budgeted for if there are no metrics? Again, the number will be PFA (Plucked From the Air). I suggest starting days with six, being half a day per month, and see how it goes.

Travel time: international

On international projects, travel is a serious issue. You will easily lose half a day travelling to the Benelux countries. If you send someone across many time zones, then recovery time becomes a concern. This cost will need to taken into account for the project. For example:

Travel to Paris: 0.5 days
Travel to Cyprus: 1 day
Travel to Tahiti: 2 days, recovery time 1 day.

Check the flight times when costing the project. If your flights are through the night, your team will arrive exhausted and will need more recovery time.

Cancellation time

Cancellation time is difficult to track. It is not an activity that is performed if a person never attends a site or a meeting: there is no activity. However, the capturing of this information is important. High incidence of cancellations will:

1. delay the project or programme, due to lost time
2. increase the costs of the project if the time cannot be re-used effectively
3. lose revenue (in the short term) as time cannot be invoiced, software installed and so forth
4. reduce the effective utilisation of an individual.

Cancellation time offers its own challenges. Clearly there is no activity if the work was cancelled at short notice. In a project, work is unlikely to be cancelled, but delayed instead.

For a consulting services business, cancellations can be costly. Without an alternative site to visit, or work to do, the revenue-earning day is lost.

The options for cancellation are:

- *Accept it.* If there is a cancellation, recognise that this is a fact of life.
- *Charge the customer* if there is insufficient notice given. Make sure that it is explicitly stated in the terms and conditions. Charging for non-attendance at a training course is not unknown. In a project environment, it is more of a balancing act. If the project or programme is worth £250,000 and for a cancellation of one day an invoice of £900 is sent, this can be seen as avaricious and not in the spirit of a long-term relationship.

There is a Sicilian expression: I don't do favours: I accumulate debts.

Instead of raising an invoice for £900, use this as leverage in the next project meeting. For example, get an invoice paid early, or a change control note signed without any 'horse trading' on the price.

When budgeting, how much revenue-earning time is lost through short-notice cancellation, which cannot be rebooked to a chargeable project? If you do not know the answer to this question then, again, a number is required. Perhaps start with one day every two months and see how it goes.

Complaints, non-conformance and no revenue

The revenue-earning capabilities did not take into account any rework, problems with installation (for example) or other items of non-conformance. From our 200 productive days, if 5% of the total had problems, then this equates to 10 days in the year.

Furthermore, we need to be cognizant of the customer who does not pay. If they have gone into liquidation, the chances of getting an invoice paid in full are unlikely. In a consulting business, it is necessary to identify a realistic amount that will be lost due to these factors.

Technology – part 2

In the early part of this section I spoke of the need to back up computers. Where there is a need to upgrade software to later releases or change operating systems, this will reduce a consultant's chargeable days. In these instances, identify the type of work and see if an IT resource dedicated to supporting the team can ensure that any downtime is reduced to a minimum.

Revised utilisation calculation

Here is a revised utilisation calculation:

Description	Days	% of Total	Class
Working days	253		
Less			
Non-productive			
Holidays	25	9.88%	Non-productive
Sickness (provision)	5	1.98%	Non-productive
Absence	1	0.40%	Non-productive
Travel time	6	2.37%	Non-productive
Christmas lost days	7	2.77%	Non-productive
Non-conformance	10	3.95%	Non-productive
Cancellation time	6	2.37%	Non-productive
Total non-productive	60	23.72%	
Investment			
Training	12	4.74%	Investment
Performance appraisals	2	0.79%	Investment
Technology	6	2.37%	Investment
Team/dept meetings	2	0.79%	Investment
Pre-sales	30	12.65%	Investment
Investment days	52	20.55%	
Revenue earning	141		

So, for a 52-week year, and 141 revenue earning days, we end up with 2.7 days per week on average being revenue earning (141/52).

Type of work considerations

Now we have 141 days to actually do some work. Achieving this can be more difficult where the work is not in whole or half-day bookings. Examples of this are chunks of work where there are not a significant number of days. Instead, work comes in the form of monthly meetings, weekly phone calls and chasing up issues. Charging for this time in quarter of an hour slots could add up to a lot of small 'chunks' of time. When presenting this on an invoice, it will look like a lawyer's bill of £31.25 for 15 minutes, £62.50 for 30 minutes (assuming £125 per hour).

In a section below, I talk about the challenge of ensuring that there is always sufficient project work coming in to book up consultants' diaries. The 141 revenue-earning days require projects and, when a project is completed, the consultant will need assigning to another immediately.

The business life cycle

The business life cycle may well impact on the work which can be booked and when. A good example is in the provision of consulting service on an enterprise resource planning system. For example:

1. Let us assume that the client wants to upgrade their accounting system from one version to another.
2. The organisation is a public limited company that run monthly accounts.
3. The monthly accounts are produced within 5 working days of the month-end.
4. Their financial year runs from January through to December.
5. In this example, Easter will be the middle weekend of April.
6. The upgrade will take 3 working days out of the month, as it is a large system, although the work starts on a Friday night with weekend work.
7. The busiest trading period is the summer months of July to September.

The upgrade cannot take place in these months.

Period	Reason
December	Year-end preparation in December ready for January – too much risk to take the system off-line
January	Year-end – need to complete annual accounts
February	Year-end completed – auditors are in reviewing the accounts
April	Easter falls in the middle of the month with 2 bank holidays (Good Friday and Easter Monday) – insufficient time in the month to take out 4 working days
June	Mid-year reporting to the Stock Exchange has to take place in July – too much risk to take the system off-line
July	Mid-year accounts have to be produced for interim reporting – too much risk to make changes to the system
August	Busy trading period – system availability required
September	Busy trading period – system availability required
November	This can be considered too close to December so is not available

So, for the 12-month, 52-week year, we can only upgrade during the middle weekends of the following months:

Month
March
May
October

In looking at the utilisation and the resource requirement policy, it is necessary to understand if there are business issues which affect your customers (whether they are internal or external). These will then affect specific skills sets within the team and the ability to ensure their time is productively used.

The IT help desk

I will use the example of an IT help desk that has to have skilled resources for every working day of the year. We will assume that there need to be 5 people on support every day to provide sufficient cover to answer calls and perform follow-up actions.

Description	Days
Working days	253
Non-productive days	
Holidays	25
Sickness (provision)	5
Absence	1
Total non-productive	31
Investment	
Training	12
Performance appraisals	2
Technology	6
Team/dept meeting	2
Total investment	22
Available days	200
IT help-desk people per day	5
Working days	253
Total	1265
Total days to be provided	1265
Divide by available days	200
Number of people required	6.3

Notes:
- Bookings for Christmas and New Year period are not applicable, as the individuals are not required to go on site.
- If you originally considered that it was 1265/253 this comes out at 5 people. The requirement for 6.3 is, of course, 26% higher than originally assumed.
- To get 0.3 of a person, you may need to consider part-time working or using a contractor.

Resource Planning & Utilisation Examples

The consultancy practice

In a consulting organisation, let us assume that there is a target to produce a gross margin of £1,500,000 per annum. The gross margin is calculated as the average daily rate charged out, less the standard cost per day for the consultant.

Initial view

Description	£	ID
Target gross margin	1,500,000	A
Average daily rate	£800	B
Standard cost per day	£250	C
Daily gross margin	£550	D = B − C
Total days	2728	E = A/D
Revenue days per consultant, (Note 1)	141	F
Consultants required (Note 2)	19.5	G = E/F
Annual turnover	£2,182,400	H = B x E

Notes:
1. The revenue days per consultant are taken from the above calculation for the consulting business.
2. The consultants required figure actually works out at 19.3 people. I have rounded this up to 19.5 assuming that there are full-time people only. Using contractors or part-time consultants would, of course, enable us to reduce the total full-time head count.
3. This does not take into account team leaders or the resource co-ordinator (or project support function).

Each consultant is able to produce £550 per day in gross margin. Assuming that the costs of team leaders and a resource coordinator is accounted for, then:

Description	£	ID
Team leader cost (x2) with a salary of £50,000 plus 50% for overheads	£150,000	J
Resource coordinator with a salary of £25,000 plus 50% for overheads	£37,500	K
Total overhead cost	£187,500	L = J x K
Gross margin per day	£550	D
Consultant days required to cover overhead cost	341	M = L/D
Revenue days per consultant	141	F
Number of additional consultants	2.42	N = M/F

Project and Programme Accounting

So, we need an additional 2.42 consultants to cover the overhead costs of 2 team leaders and a resource coordinator. The 0.42 could come from contracting out work.

The solutions business

In the previous example, the aim was to produce £1.5m in gross margin through consulting activity. For a business that sells software, software maintenance as well as services, the use of the consultants will be different. Again the utilisation is calculated as before, except the pre-sales entry is removed.

Description	Days	% of Total	Class
Working days	253		
Less			
Non-productive			
Holidays	25	9.88%	Non-productive
Sickness (provision)	5	1.98%	Non-productive
Absence	1	0.40%	Non-productive
Travel time	6	2.37%	Non-productive
Christmas lost days	7	2.77%	Non-productive
Non-conformance	10	3.95%	Non-productive
Cancellation time	6	2.37%	Non-productive
Total non-productive	60	23.72%	
Investment			
Training	12	4.74%	Investment
Performance appraisals	2	0.79%	Investment
Technology	6	2.37%	Investment
Team/dept meetings	2	0.79%	Investment
Pre-sales	30	12.65%	Investment
Investment days	52	20.55%	

The pre-sales work should give rise to software and software maintenance revenue when the contract is won.

If the revenue relationship in projects is

Description	Value	% of Total	Gross margin
Average project value	£200,000		
Software revenue	£90,000	45%	£45,000
Consulting revenue	£90,000	45%	£63,600
Maintenance revenue	£20,000	10%	£10,000
			£118,600

consulting revenue of £90,000 on a daily rate of £850 per day is 106 days. With a standard daily cost of £250 per day, the margin is £850 – £250 x 106 = £63,600.

Now, to produce a total gross margin of £1.5m:

Description	Value	ID
Total gross margin target	£1,500,000	A
Average project gross margin	£118,600	B
Number of projects (Note 1)	13	C = A/B
Average project days (Note 2)	106	D
Total days sold	1378	E = D x C
Revenue-earning days (Note 3)	141	
Number of consultants (Note 4)	10	

Notes:
1. The number of projects is actually 12.65.
2. The average project days is calculated above in the revenue relationship.
3. Although the productive days are 171, this includes the pre-sales time to get us the software and maintenance revenue as well as the project revenue. We still need to get the business, so I have chosen the 141 as the productive days that can be charged to the customer.
4. The division of 1378 by 141 gives 9.77 people, so this is rounded up to 10.

Value billing

There were some businesses, during the dot com era, which paid for their services through the issuing of shares or share options. The idea was that the success of the business produced share price growth, thereby rewarding the supplier and sharing the risk of the business.

I visited a company who were in the legal services and wealth management business. Their legal team were expert at finding ways of reducing a person's income tax liability, or other ways of keeping money.

They raised invoices, not based on the amount of time spent, but rather as a percentage of the total savings made. If the customer saved £250,000 from the work, then the bill might be 10% at £25,000.

This was objected to in some instances, as the amount of work done could amount to perhaps one hour! It wasn't that the customer didn't want to save £225,000 (being the £250,000 less the 10% bill of £25,000), but rather that the £25,000 was not perceived as value for money. As Roger Dawson says in his 'Secrets of power negotiation' audiotapes, 'the value of goods and services diminishes soon after they are received'.

If you can follow a value-billing model, good luck!

A model for resource planning
Total working days and non-productive days

Resource Planning Model							Non Productive			
Team	<Team Name>									
Productive Days Calculation			Days in		Bank	Working	Annual	Sickness	Absence	Non-Productive
Employee Name Timesheet Code		Count	Year	Weekends	Holidays	Days	Holiday	(Provision)		Total
<Employee : 25 days hol>		1	365	104	8	253	25	5	1	31
<Employee : 25 days hol>		1	365	104	8	253	25	5	1	31
<Employee : 30 days hol>		1	365	104	8	253	30	5	1	36
<Spare>			0	0	0	0	0	0	0	0
<Spare>			0	0	0	0	0	0	0	0
<Spare>			0	0	0	0	0	0	0	0
<Spare>			0	0	0	0	0	0	0	0
<Spare>			0	0	0	0	0	0	0	0
<Spare>			0	0	0	0	0	0	0	0
Totals		3				759	80	15	3	98

Investment days

Resource Planning Model			Non Productive		Investment					
Team	<Team Name>									
Productive Days Calculation			Working Days	Total		Performance		Dept & Team	Total	
Employee Name		Count	in Year		Training	Appraisals	Technology	Meetings	Investment	
<Employee : 25 days hol>		1	253	31	12	2	6	2	22	
<Employee : 25 days hol>		1	253	31	12	2	6	2	22	
<Employee : 30 days hol>		1	253	36	12	2	6	2	22	
<Spare>			0	0	0	0	0	0	0	
<Spare>			0	0	0	0	0	0	0	
<Spare>			0	0	0	0	0	0	0	
<Spare>			0	0	0	0	0	0	0	
<Spare>			0	0	0	0	0	0	0	
<Spare>			0	0	0	0	0	0	0	
Totals		3		98	36	6	18	6	66	

Productive days calculated

Resource Planning Model								
Team	<Team Name>							
Productive Days Calculation			Days in	Working days	Non Productive	Investment	Productive	Utilisation %
Employee Name		Count	Year	in Year	Total	Total	Days	
<Employee : 25 days hol>		1	365	253	31	22	200	79.05%
<Employee : 25 days hol>		1	365	253	31	22	200	79.05%
<Employee : 30 days hol>		1	365	253	36	22	195	77.08%
<Spare>			0	0	0	0	0	
<Spare>			0	0	0	0	0	
<Spare>			0	0	0	0	0	
<Spare>			0	0	0	0	0	
<Spare>			0	0	0	0	0	
<Spare>			0	0	0	0	0	
Totals		3	1095	759	98	66	595	78.39%

The consultancy model

The Consultancy Model Employee Name	Count	Working Days in Year	Original Productive Days	Less Travel Time	Lost Days	Non Conformance	Cancellations	Pre-Sales	Revenue Days	Utilisation %
<Employee : 25 days hol>	1	253	200	6	7	10	6	30	141	55.73%
<Employee : 25 days hol>	1	253	200	6	7	10	6	30	141	55.73%
<Employee : 30 days hol>	1	253	195	6	7	10	6	30	136	53.75%
<Spare>		0	0	0	0	0	0	0	0	
<Spare>		0	0	0	0	0	0	0	0	
<Spare>		0	0	0	0	0	0	0	0	
<Spare>		0	0	0	0	0	0	0	0	
<Spare>		0	0	0	0	0	0	0	0	
<Spare>		0	0	0	0	0	0	0	0	
Totals	3	759	595	98	0	0	0	0	418	55.07%

Example chargeable utilisation levels

The amount of chargeable work that can be performed will vary from organisation to organisation. This is known as utilisation analysis. The aim in maximising utilisation levels is to ensure that, when a project finishes, there is another one lined up to put people on to. This is easier said than done.

Utilisation in a small consultancy

Where the consulting operation is one or a few people, then there is unlikely to be a sales function. Maximising utilisation will require working every day that is on offer. So, if a person is working on a large contract, which has a rolling renewal every three months, they will not go looking for other work in the meantime.

Once the contract has finished, unless there was sufficient notice to find other work, then the time becomes free and the bidding for new business begins again.

Therefore, their utilisation graph is likely to look like this:

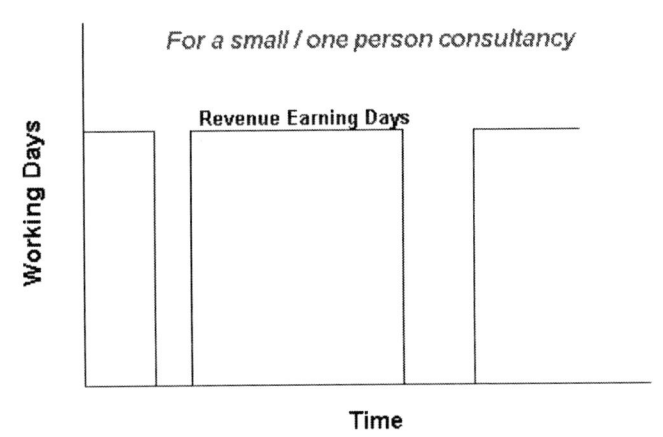

where the utilisation level is either high, or not at all.

Hint: If you are thinking of 'going it alone', make sure you are clear on how you are going to get work. A few weeks of no money coming in and still bills to pay is not pleasant.

Utilisation in a medium-sized consultancy

Here the problems are similar to the small organisation. However, if the business has a sales team or is perhaps part of a group of companies with a dedicated customer base, then the completion of one project should not have such an enormous impact on the overall fee earners.

The difficulty comes where there are perhaps two or three large contracts running concurrently. Should they come to a close around the same time, then many consultants will come free and work has to be found for them.

Their utilisation graph is likely to be as below:

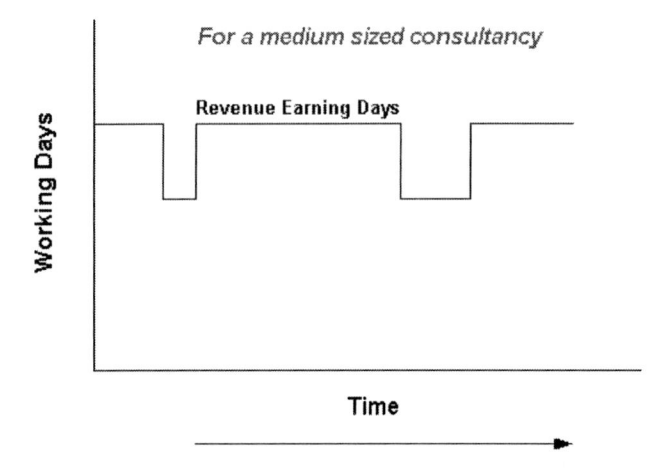

For a medium sized consultancy

Revenue Earning Days

Working Days

Time

Here the calculation of total revenue earning days is taken across a team of people. In the previous example, either the consultant was working or not. For the above, a few lost days to no booking will reduce overall levels of utilisation. The net effect is a dip from the norm.

Utilisation in a large consulting firm

For large consulting firms who undertake many projects and have large teams working across many sectors, the completion of one project is likely to have a small effect on overall utilisation levels. Their utilisation graph would look like:

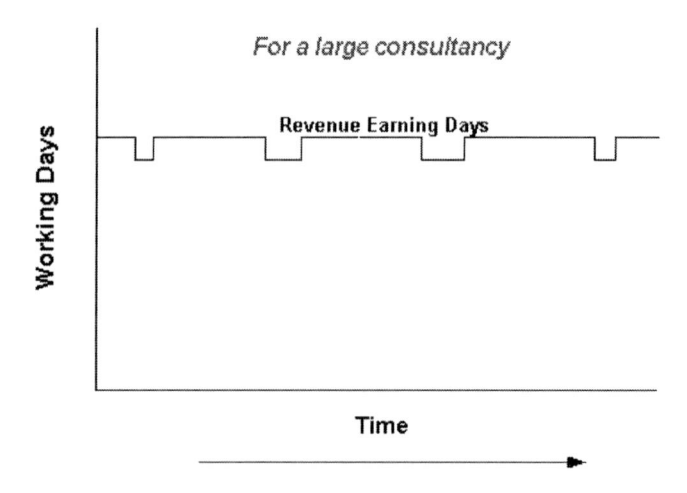

For a large consultancy

Revenue Earning Days

Working Days

Time

Resource Planning & Utilisation Examples

Again, the completion of one project, especially a large project using many of the business resources, will have an impact on overall utilisation levels. However, the calculation is across a large group of people, so the overall utilisation levels remain high.

Calculating the number of transactions

In implementing a system, it is important to calculate the number of transactions which are to be entered. For the time recording, the start point is the utilisation calculation. This has been enhanced below to give a likely average number of transactions for each of the key elements.

Description	Days	Likely average	Total transactions
Working days	253		
Less			
Non-productive			
Holidays	25	1.5 per day	38
Sickness (provision)	5	1 per day	5
Absence	1	1 per day	1
Travel time	6	1 per half day	12
Christmas lost days	7	1 per day	7
Non-conformance	10	1 per half day	20
Cancellation time	6	1 per day	6
Total non-productive	60		89
Investment			
Training	12	1 per day	12
Performance appraisals	2	1 per half day	4
Technology	6	2 per month	24
Team/dept meetings	2	1 per half day	4
Pre-sales	30	1 per day	30
Investment days	52		74
Revenue earning	141	2 per day	282
			445

Notes:
1. Holidays allows for a combination of full and half days
2. Performance appraisals assumes 4 x 0.5 days
3. Technology assumes 6 days across 12 months at 2 entries per month
4. Team/dept meetings assumes 4 meetings of half a day
5. Pre-sales assumes that each pre-sales visit takes a day

6. The revenue days are taken assuming that, on average, there are two separate activities in the project plan that are worked on. This will vary from organisation to organisation.
7. If the type of work is not in daily or part-day slots, eg, charging by the hour or part thereof, then there will be many more entries in the timesheet system.

Depending on the size of your organisation, the estimated number of timesheet entries per annum would work out as:

Number of people	Avg no of entries	Total per annum	For 3 years
25	445	13,375	40,125
50	445	26,750	80,250
75	445	40,125	120,375
100	445	53,500	160,500
125	445	66,875	200,625
150	445	80,250	240,750
200	445	107,000	321,000
250	445	133,750	401,250
300	445	160,500	481,500

Very quickly the numbers build up, hence the importance of getting the data structure correct in the first instance.

Conclusion

In resource planning, you will need to define the purpose of the individuals in your team. For example:

1. Is it to charge for every day possible that a consultant performs? – This is the pure consulting model.
2. Is it to model the days on the help desk, as in the example, to identify what the optimum level of resource is?
3. Is it to maximise overall revenue? Eg, in a software and services business, a senior consultant could be very effective at defining business solutions, opening up the sales process and getting in orders of £100,000 from an investment of 10 days pre-sales. Here the effectiveness of the resource is to produce revenue – albeit via a different mechanism from straight invoicing for time.
4. Is it to maximise revenue through value billing? In this instance, there is unlikely to be a correlation between time spent and income received.

Levels of utilisation will vary from person to person and organisation to organisation. I spoke to a former director of one of the big six consultancies (when they still existed). His view was that 65% of 253 days was normal for their consultants. This calculates to 165 chargeable days per year.

Finally, if you incorrectly calculate the time it takes to perform a project, then:

a) If the calculation is below the required level of activity, the customer is unlikely to want to accept the additional time (unless it can be shown that it was their fault). This will depress consulting income and, where the people are to be put on to another project, interrupt follow-on work.
b) If the calculation is too high, the project or programme will finish early, leaving consulting resources idle.

Getting the estimating correct is therefore of high importance.

Section Three: Reporting

ANALYSING THE DATA
Introduction
Software systems should come with a number of listing reports, showing time spent by employee, by project, by programme, with resources expended, expenses incurred and so forth. What we are interested in is the data, in order to 'mine' for information[1].

Analysis falls into two categories:

- Operational improvements: those that focus on reducing non-conformance, making the business more efficient
- Strategic improvements: for example, about deciding whether the type of project or programme should be pursued.

Making sense of the data
Start with profiling the data. If you have not done this in the past, I suggest you look to answer the following questions.

---

1. It is important that conclusions can be drawn from the data – using the 'Law of Large Numbers'. Suppose you toss a coin over and over. 'The Law of Large Numbers does not tell you that the average of your throws will approach 50% as you increase the number of throws. Rather the Law states that increasing the number of throws will correspondingly increase the 50% by less than some stated amount, no matter how small. All the Law tells us is that the average of a large number of throws will be more likely than the average of a small number of throws to differ from the true average by less than some stated amount.' (From *Against the gods – the remarkable story of risk*. See Bibliography for details.)

I emphasise this point. In presenting your findings, there will be numbers which individuals will find embarrassing. Statements such as 'No, I can find examples of where the values differ from your findings' will be made as a justification for ridiculing or suggesting that what you state is incorrect. Be prepared for this response. You will need to be able to defend your figures.

Analysis	Use of information
Operational improvements	
Where is the time going, by activity?	To understand the nature of the work performed and skills required.
What are the major groupings, if any, of projects, programmes, people, activities?	To look for common issues, and an appreciation of the business.
What is the average size of project (in days performed, in revenue)?	To look for common issues, and an appreciation of the business.
What is the average size of programme (in days performed, in revenue)?	To look for common issues, and an appreciation of the business.
How long (from start date to completion date) is the average project or programme?	To enable better business planning, programme and project planning
What is the average/maximum/median number of days between the date of the work and the date the time was invoiced?	This is especially important for revenue planning, and understanding the operational efficiency of your business. (It will need to be analysed by contract type.)
What numbers of days are there between the date of the work and the date the timesheet was entered?	This is a key indicator of an employee's efficiency. It impacts on the reporting, invoicing and all subsequent functions.
What is the number of days from invoice date to cash received date?	This is important for cash-flow planning, contract style, operational processes.
On overruns, are there any areas that stand out (by project, by person, by activity, by customer, by product, by project manager)?	You can then focus your management effort on addressing these.
Which project manager produced the most/least revenue?	Reward the achievers; focus on the non-achiever.
Which consultant produced the most/least revenue?	Reward the achievers; focus on the non-achiever.
Which consultancy team produced the most/least revenue?	Reward the team leader; focus on the non-achiever.
Which consultant performed the most days (excluding non-productive time)?	If this is not the person who produced the most revenue, you need to understand why not.

Analysis	Use of information
Operational Improvements (cont'd)	
What is the average revenue produced by a consultant (by quarter, six months, year)?	Better business planning.
What is the actual utilisation against budget (by person, by project, by programme)?	Understand the efficacy and efficiency of the team. Tells you how good your budgeting is. Also, what is the link to core competencies.
If you are invoicing/costing by days, how many hours have been performed?	If the total hours/7.5 (or whatever your working hours in a day are) is materially more than the days charged, next time charge by the hour, not the day.
What is the level of cancellation time?	If there is a significant amount of cancellation time, charge a cancellation fee or look at how you negotiate the contract.
Does one customer's project or programme have a significant impact on the revenue stream?	One customer is too powerful. The programme when finishing will cause a lack of work.
On a project or programme, what is the % of revenue between time and non-time-related items (for example consultancy revenue compared to the total of hardware, software, etc.)?	Looking for patterns will assist in understanding the business. Likewise, with 'what if' analysis, it is possible to profile the effect of, eg, lowering software prices.
What level of overtime was performed?	Significant amounts of overtime tire people. To perform at their best, they need sleep and to have a balanced lifestyle. Use this to understand the deficiencies from planning, forecasting and expectation management.
What was the overtime cost?	Supporting argument when trying to bring about changes in planning and forecasting techniques.
What level of expenses were incurred on the project or programme?	Should expenses be recovered from the customer?
How effective was the expense recovery?	Operational effectiveness of procedures for expense tracking and recovery.

Analysis	Use of information
Operational Improvements (cont'd)	
Does the policy of expense recovery require changing based on geographical location of work?	Using the field, geographical location, it is possible to calculate the average distance from your offices to the sites which are worked at. By understanding this, you can see the impact on the project team, as well as the expense implications.
What use was made of taxis?	In central London it is easy to jump into a taxi but more cost-effective to use the underground or bus. Are employees able to change their habits to reduce costs?
How much use is made of hotels, air travel?	Booking hotels and flights takes significant time. On the next project or programme, negotiate into the contract that the customer arranges hotels, air travel, etc.
Are there any significant problems with a supplier?	Use the information to negotiate lower costs/better payment terms.
What is the number of days between the date the order was placed (from the customer) to: • when the project or programme started (first timesheet date) • when the first installation began • when the invoice was first/last raised • when the project or programme completed?	To calculate the manufacturing cycle time effectiveness[2].

---

2. Manufacturing cycle effectiveness (MCE): a method used by manufacturing organisations to move to just-in-time production flow processes. The MCE is defined as follows:

$$\text{MCE} = \frac{\text{processing time}}{\text{throughput time}}$$

The theory behind the MCE calculation is that all time, other than processing time, that is time used for inspections, reworking defective items, moving items from one process to the next, and having items wait until processed at the next stage, is waste or non-value-added time. (From the book, *Cost & Effect*. See Bibliography for details.)

In the software requirements, there is a requirement to store the initial customer order date. This can be used to calculate the time through each of the stages. By reducing the total delivery time, the cash collection time is increased and the chance of change interrupting our project or programme drops. Furthermore, in reviewing the end-to-end process, if this can be improved upon, the organisation becomes more competitive.

Analysis	Use of information
Strategic review	
Which customer spent the most with you?	Buy them lunch!
Which customer produced the least in profitable business?	Get them to go to your competitor!
What is the total revenue from change control notes raised?	Better understanding of additional revenue opportunities. If there is only cost, then model what areas are going wrong and feed back into the project or programme life cycle.
What is the total time from change control notes raised?	Better understanding of additional revenue opportunities. If there is only cost, then model what areas are going wrong and feed back into the project or programme life cycle.
What activities, if any, are typically subcontracted out?	Decide if this is becoming a core competency. Subcontracting has its risks, as individuals can leave at short notice. Perhaps it is work which needs to be performed by a PAYE employee.
Are there indicators from the non-productive time analysis?	Examples to look for are excessive travelling time, computer failure, etc. Excessive travelling time to remote projects will not show as a project cost, just an overhead cost. Perhaps the time should be held against the project to get a truer reflection on total cost.
Which are most profitable as a % of turnover?	Is it worth selling more of these?
Which projects and programmes are least profitable as a % of turnover?	Is it worth dropping this as a service offering?
What is the total number of different programme offerings?	Do more programme services need to be developed?
What is the total number of different project offerings?	Do more project services need to be developed?
What changes occurred in the budgets from inception to completion?	This is an important indicator to show the change in programme or project scope. Many changes in budget indicate a moving target, which is difficult to control.
What discounts off list price (should there be one) were offered to obtain the business?	This report will require some work. It will be necessary to compare the prices charged for capital and non-capital items (such as consultancy) against the published price list at the time. However, it is an important indicator to show whether the prices are being discounted heavily to get business or whether the current pricing policy is correct.

How to analyse?

The heavy emphasis earlier on in the book was to ensure that the data, which is analysed, is in a commonly coded, well structured, cross-project and cross-programme analysable form.

In looking at the data structure, there are the areas of:

- employee time (days/hours)
- subcontractor time (days/hours)
- receivables/sales
- payables/purchases
- budget versus actual.

Each of these should be analysed by:

- project
- programme
- project versus project
- programme versus programme

with sub-analysis by activity or group of activities to allow for drill-down analysis

Arrange the data into a list form. My personal preference is to use Microsoft Excel. The pivot table analysis is excellent (although there are limits to the number of rows of data which can be analysed, so check with your version of Excel first). I recommend you spend time learning this feature. In one hour you can get a good feel for the functionality.

Look at the above analysis areas and decide which one or ones are the key performance indicators for your business. For example, the number of days to produce an invoice is important and needs to be watched. More important is the actual versus budget days utilisation on a month-by-month and year-to-date basis.

The suggested analysis above is to give a feel for this type of modelling.

Example reports

When designing the system, it is important to identify what type of reporting is required. With pivot tables and dynamic modelling tools, the data can be cut and sliced in many ways.

There are still some standard reports which will be required, including the following.

Customer revenue

This is a report of total revenue, costs and profit.

	Revenue	Cost	Profit	Profit %
Customer 1	999.99	999.99	999.99	n%
Customer 2	999.99	999.99	999.99	n%
Customer 3	999.99	999.99	999.99	n%
Customer 4	999.99	999.99	999.99	n%
Total	999.99	999.99	999.99	n%

Days budget analysis

This is a report of days budgeted versus days actual.

	Days budget	Days actual	Variance	Var %
Project 1	999.99	999.99	999.99	n%
Project 2	999.99	999.99	999.99	n%
Project 3	999.99	999.99	999.99	n%
Project 4	999.99	999.99	999.99	n%
Total	999.99	999.99	999.99	n%

Revenue budget analysis

This is a report of revenue budgeted versus revenue actual.

	Revenue budget	Revenue actual	Variance	Var %
Project 1	999.99	999.99	999.99	n%
Project 2	999.99	999.99	999.99	n%
Project 3	999.99	999.99	999.99	n%
Project 4	999.99	999.99	999.99	n%
Total	999.99	999.99	999.99	n%

Project costs

This is a report of project costs. For an explanation on soft and hard commitments see the payables chapter, starting on page 59.

	Budgeted costs A	'Soft' commitments B	'Hard' commitments C	Costs to date D	Total costs E = B+C+D	Variance against budget A – E
Project 1	999.99	999.99	999.99	999.99	999.99	999.99
Project 2	999.99	999.99	999.99	999.99	999.99	999.99
Project 3	999.99	999.99	999.99	999.99	999.99	999.99
Project 4	999.99	999.99	999.99	999.99	999.99	999.99
Total	999.99	999.99	999.99	999.99	999.99	999.99

Profit budget analysis

This is a report of profit budgeted versus profit actual.

	Profit budget	Profit actual	Variance	Var %
Project 1	999.99	999.99	999.99	n%
Project 2	999.99	999.99	999.99	n%
Project 3	999.99	999.99	999.99	n%
Project 4	999.99	999.99	999.99	n%
Total	999.99	999.99	999.99	n%

Project and Programme Accounting

Project progress
This is a report of project progress.

	Revenue to date	Revenue forecast	Revenue budget	Revenue budget	Var %
Project 1	999.99	999.99	999.99	999.99	n%
Project 2	999.99	999.99	999.99	999.99	n%
Project 3	999.99	999.99	999.99	999.99	n%
Project 4	999.99	999.99	999.99	999.99	n%
Total	999.99	999.99	999.99	999.99	n%

For each of the above reports, check that it can be provided electronically with drill-down capabilities.

Publishing the reports
In the time-recording chapter there is an entry about publishing the reports and then getting negative feedback. When a system is first implemented, especially if no meaningful numbers have been produced in the past, then it is likely that there will be a few surprises. Expectation management will be important, especially when working with senior management.

Publishing utilisation figures with employee comparison is likely to provoke a reaction. I have come across denial of the figures, comments that they should not be published due to people's sensitivities, and just plain hostility. (For the cynically minded, you might think this is 'white-collar' resentment at the introduction of 'blue-collar' productivity measures.)

What about VAT?
In the sales ledger, the customer's numbers will include VAT (unless it is an overseas customer). At the current VAT rate of 17.5% this will inflate the figures considerably. The majority of the reporting needs to be excluding VAT. The exception is cash collection where the amount received will include VAT.

This needs to be taken into account when analysing invoice totals. It should be possible to get at the data exclusive of VAT. Ask the supplier of your system for a copy of the data model and field layouts.

Summary
It is only through the modelling and reviewing of data that the nature of the business can be understood. The numbers will support any change proposals in the way of running a project or programme.

Focusing on operational improvements should enable higher profitability as a percentage of turnover. Small improvements such as an additional chargeable day per consultant per quarter soon add up (eg, 4 days per annum at £1,000 per day, times 20 consultants equals £80,000). Furthermore, in the negotiation stage of new contracts, with a strong comprehension of what has happened in the past, the lessons learned can be combined with the analysis to enable more competitive quotes to be delivered.

Section Four: Defining and implementing a system

IMPLEMENTATION ISSUES
Introduction
For any packaged solution, there will be defined stages such as project initiation, software installation, end-user training and so forth.

The purpose of this chapter is not to define these, but to look at the specific points to take into account when implementing a project or programme accounting system.

The items are:

1. List the projects and programmes
2. Identify the runners, repeaters and strangers
3. Create the data model
4. Identify the component parts
5. Identify the information flow
6. Identify the user locations and what access they will need to the system
7. Create the employee budget model
8. Identify the 'dummy' projects
9. Develop the utilisation class list
10. Develop the entity list and coding structure
11. Define the employee costs
12. Define the charges
13. Identify the purchase costs
14. Review the contract terms
15. Define a day
16. Define the data requirements
17. Define the reporting requirements
18. Define the outputs
19. Look at the cultural issues
20. Who are the resistors to change
21. What is the technological infrastructure requirement

Once you have this information, then the software requirements can be deduced.

1. List projects and programmes
Types of projects and programmes
Prepare a list of the different types of projects and programmes. For example: the project list for a professional services firm implementing financial accounting solutions could say:

- New system implementation
- End-user training
- Installing a single module
- Troubleshooting
- Upgrading systems from one release to another
- Ad hoc consulting.

Customers
Prepare the following lists:

- How many customers are there?
- For each customer, what is the number of projects and programmes that are currently active?

Active projects and programmes
Taking the information derived from the above two lists, identify:

- the average number of open projects and programmes per customer
- the average number of open projects and programmes for your company as a whole
- whether project managers and programme managers need to be restricted to only assigned jobs.

2. Divide this list into runners, repeaters and strangers
Take the results from above and put each project into the relevant programme group (runner, repeater or stranger).

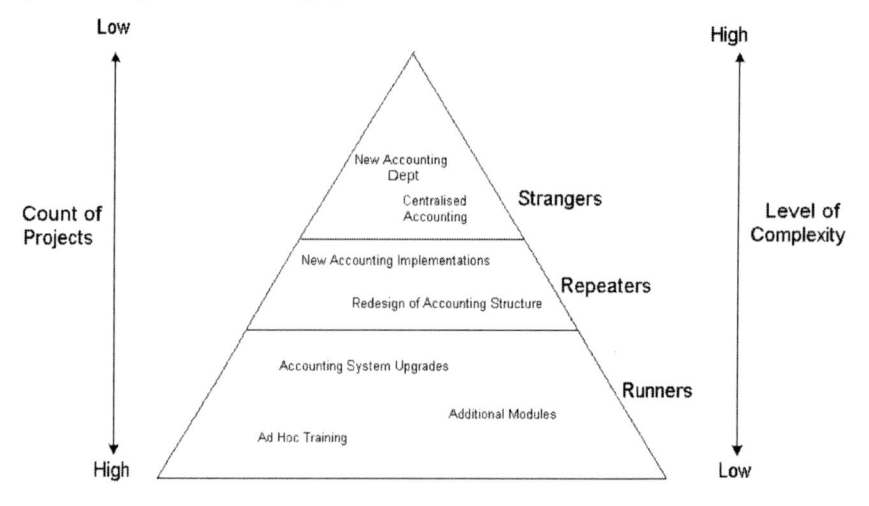

When a project or programme is created, it should be classified according to one of these three criteria. This is for subsequent analysis of the data.

3. Create the data model

Now that you have the list of project and programme types, and where they fit in the pyramid, the hierarchy of relationships should be defined.

This first one is used when reviewing the implementation of a system to check that the reporting tools can show a customer who has one or more projects and programmes.

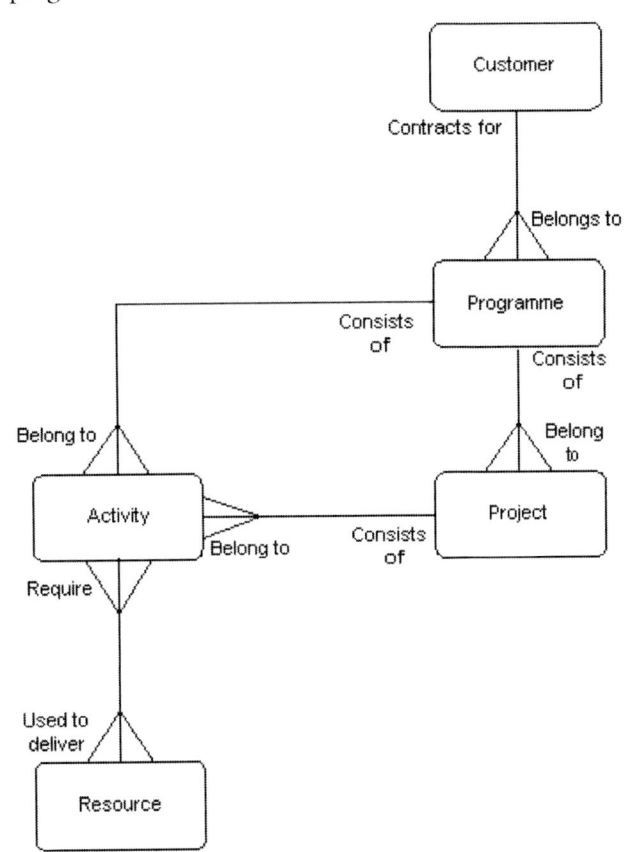

Consider how this will be stored in the system that is in use, or is to be implemented.

Project and Programme Accounting

The second one you can use to test that the reporting will enable the drawing together of like projects for multiple customers.

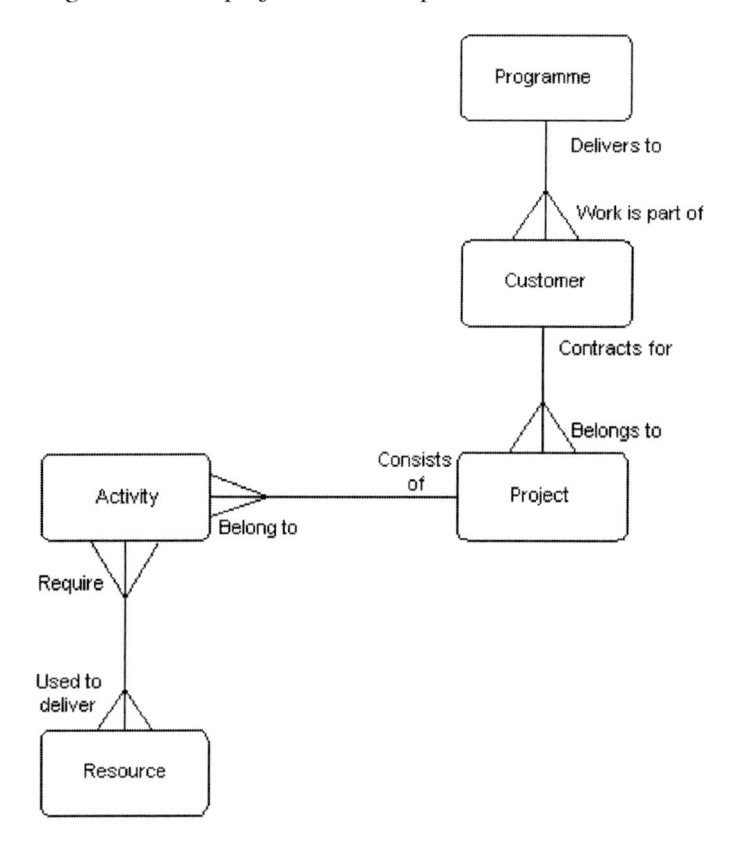

```
                    ┌───────────┐
                    │ Programme │
                    └───────────┘
                          │ Delivers to
                          △ Work is part of
                    ┌───────────┐
                    │ Customer  │
                    └───────────┘
                          │ Contracts for
                          △ Belongs to
                 Consists  ┌─────────┐
┌──────────┐       of     │ Project │
│ Activity │◁─────────────└─────────┘
└──────────┘  Belong to
     │
     │ Require
     │
     △ Used to deliver
┌──────────┐
│ Resource │
└──────────┘
```

Consider how this will be stored in the system that is in use, or is to be implemented.

4. Identify the component parts

For the projects and programmes in your portfolio, identify the component parts, ie, what makes up a project's costs and revenue.

For example, draw up a hierarchical structure:

Programme & Project Budgets

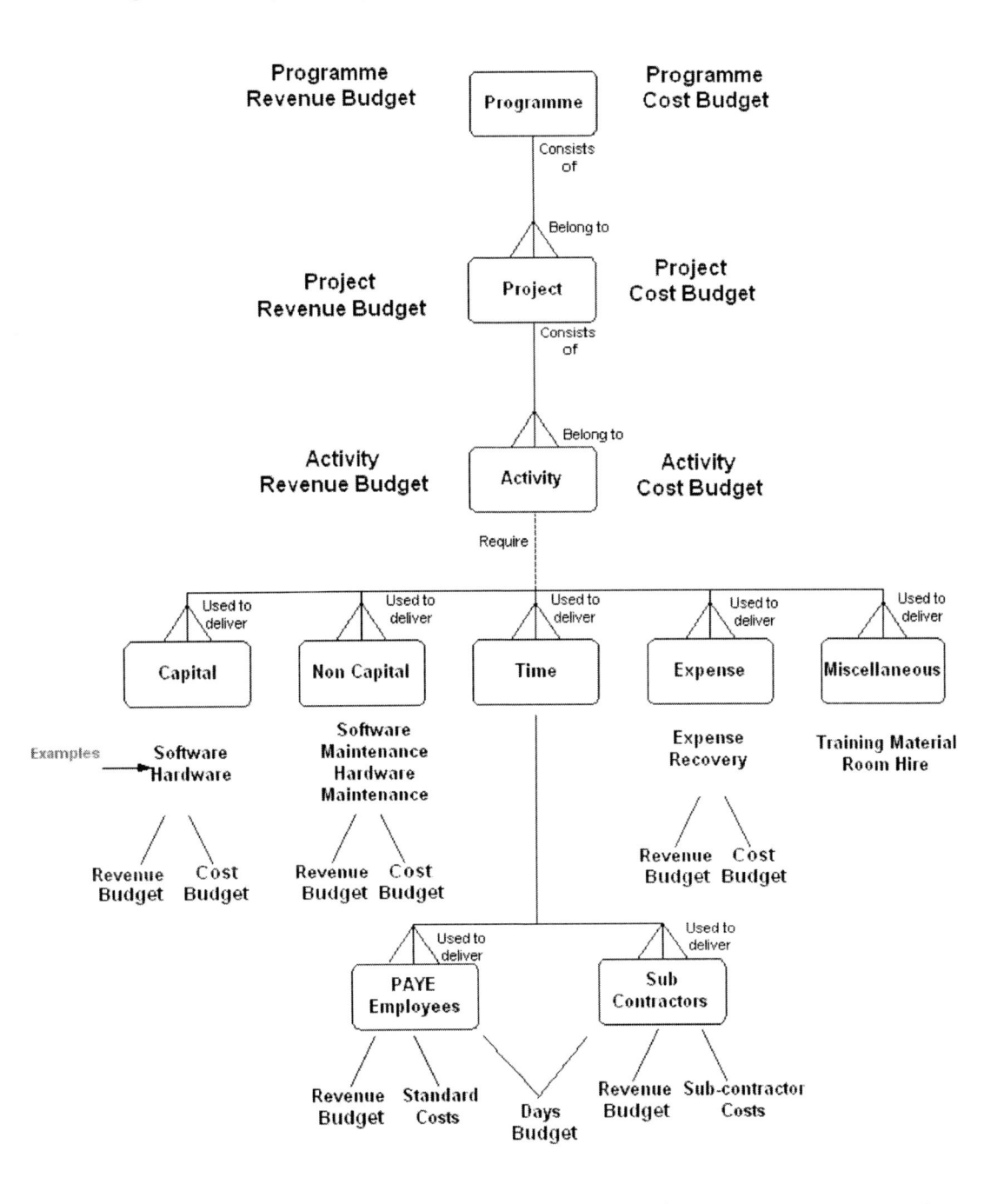

```
                    Programme                              Programme
                    Revenue Budget        [Programme]      Cost Budget
                                              │
                                         Consists of
                                              │
                                         Belong to
                                              │
                    Project                               Project
                    Revenue Budget         [Project]      Cost Budget
                                              │
                                         Consists of
                                              │
                                         Belong to
                                              │
                    Activity                              Activity
                    Revenue Budget        [Activity]      Cost Budget
                                              │
                                           Require
```

Used to deliver: Capital | Non Capital | Time | Expense | Miscellaneous

Examples →
- Capital: Software, Hardware → Revenue Budget, Cost Budget
- Non Capital: Software Maintenance, Hardware Maintenance → Revenue Budget, Cost Budget
- Time → Used to deliver: PAYE Employees, Sub Contractors
  - PAYE Employees → Revenue Budget, Standard Costs, Days Budget
  - Sub Contractors → Revenue Budget, Sub-contractor Costs
- Expense: Expense Recovery → Revenue Budget, Cost Budget
- Miscellaneous: Training Material, Room Hire

135

Project and Programme Accounting

5. Identify the information flow

Define the flow of information for your projects and programmes and optimise it (to develop standard costs for payroll). For example:

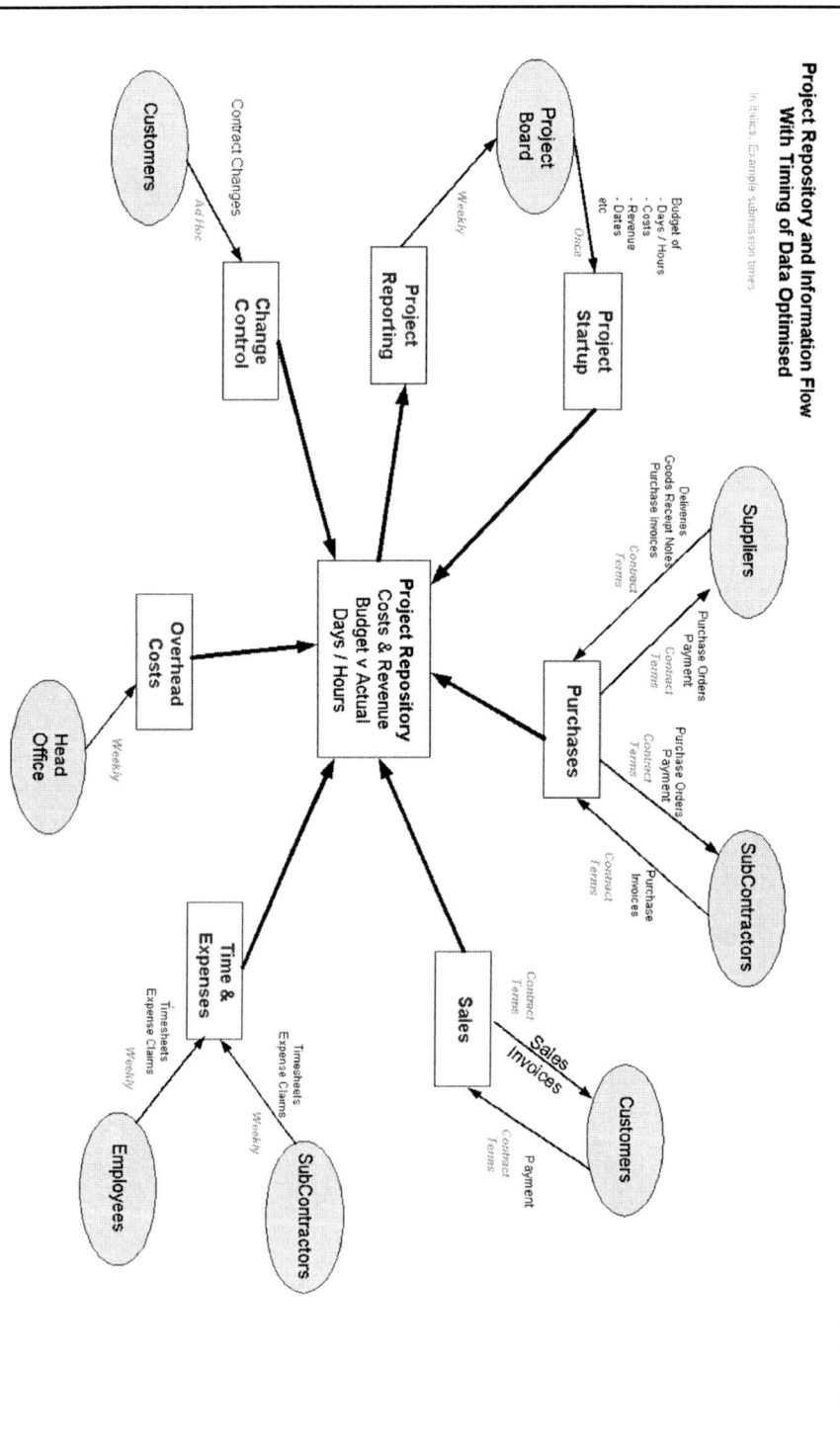

Project Repository and Information Flow With Timing of Data Optimised

In italics: Example submission times

```
                                                    Budget of
                                                    - Days / Hours
                            ┌──────────┐            - Costs
                            │ Project  │            - Revenue
                            │  Board   │            - Dates
                            └──────────┘              etc
                               │    ▲
                        Weekly │    │ Once
                               ▼    │
     ┌──────────┐        ┌──────────┐         ┌──────────┐          Deliveries
     │Customers │        │ Project  │         │ Project  │          Goods Receipt Notes
     └──────────┘        │Reporting │         │ Startup  │          Purchase Invoices
           │             └──────────┘         └──────────┘             Contract
Contract   │                   ▲                    │                   Terms
Changes    ▼                   │                    │               ┌──────────┐
     ┌──────────┐              │                    ▼               │Suppliers │
     │ Change   │──────────────┼────────┐                           └──────────┘
Ad Hoc│ Control │              │        │                                ▲
     └──────────┘              │        ▼                                │
                         ┌──────────────────┐      Purchase Orders       │
                         │Project Repository│      Payment               │
                         │Costs & Revenue   │◄─────Contract              │
                         │Budget v Actual   │      Terms                 │
     ┌──────────┐        │  Days / Hours    │                     ┌──────────┐
     │ Overhead │───────►│                  │                     │Purchases │
     │  Costs   │        └──────────────────┘                     └──────────┘
     └──────────┘              ▲      ▲                            Purchase Orders
           ▲                   │      │                            Payment
    Weekly │                   │      │                            Contract Terms
           │                   │      │
     ┌──────────┐              │      │                           ┌──────────────┐
     │  Head    │              │      │                           │SubContractors│
     │  Office  │              │      │                           └──────────────┘
     └──────────┘              │      │                            Purchase Invoices
                               │      │                            Contract Terms
                         ┌──────────┐ │
                         │ Time &   │ │         ┌──────────┐      Contract Terms
                         │ Expenses │ │         │  Sales   │◄─────
                         └──────────┘ └────────►└──────────┘      Sales Invoices
                           ▲      ▲                  ▲                │
                Timesheets │      │ Timesheets       │                ▼
                Expense    │      │ Expense Claims   │           ┌──────────┐
                Claims     │Weekly│  Weekly          │ Payment   │Customers │
                           │      │                  └───────────│          │
                    ┌──────────┐ ┌──────────────┐                └──────────┘
                    │Employees │ │SubContractors│                 Contract Terms
                    └──────────┘ └──────────────┘
```

Process changes may be required to ensure that requisite data is captured. The first place will be project start-up. Try and design a solution that starts at the pre-sales process and works all the way through to invoice production and cash payment.

136

6. User locations and access required

List each of the users of the system and where they are located. For each user identify which system features they require.

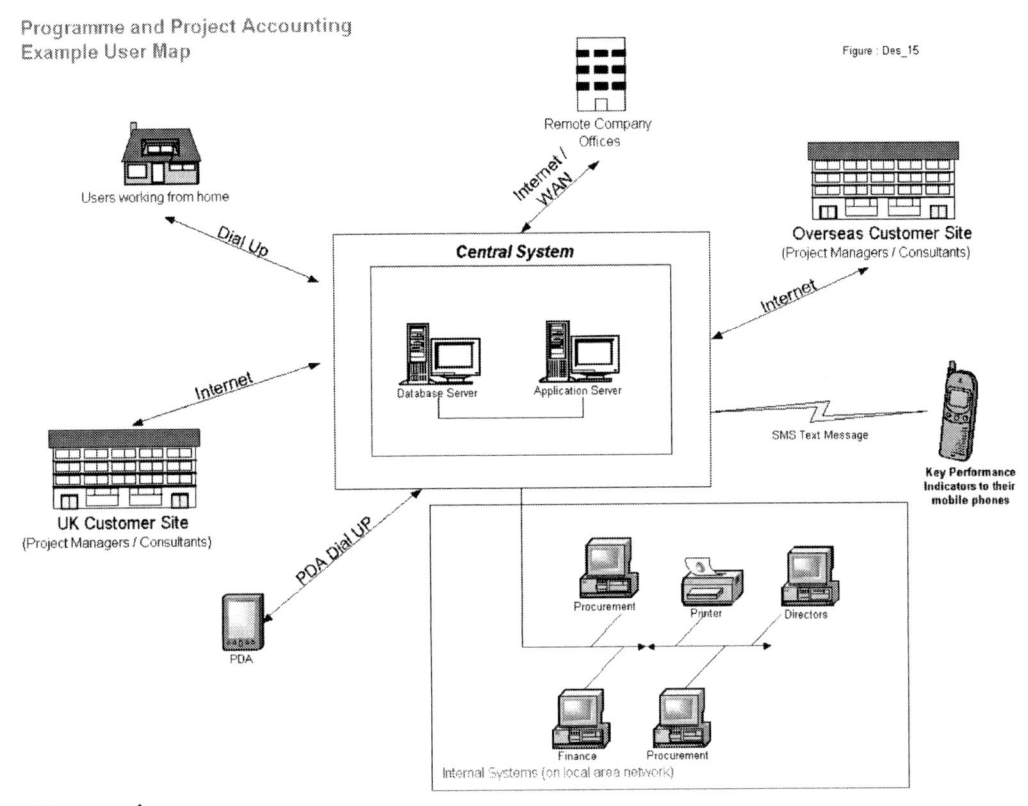

Programme and Project Accounting
Example User Map

Figure : Des_15

Here we have:

1. Users working from home – possibly timesheet & expense entry
2. Users working at a customer's site – timesheet & expense entry, getting sign-off of goods received
3. Remote company offices – which could be on the WAN and are seen as part of the local area network
4. Overseas sites where project managers and consultants are working. The only possible access out of their site might be through the Internet
5. An internal system – on which the relevant software is installed
6. Remote users who want key performance indicator information on their mobile phones – such as total invoices raised for the previous week.

Notes
1. Users working from home may need data-capture facilities (such as timesheets and expenses) while disconnected from the network
2. Users working on a customer's site may only have Internet access, so any system might require publishing through an Internet browser.

Project and Programme Accounting

7. Create the employee budget model

In developing your utilisation analysis, you need a starting point and that is the budget of employee time. This can be created using Microsoft Excel which will ease the calculation of the totals by employee, by project type and by department.

The details below will enable you to determine the productive days. (See the resource planning and utilisation chapter, page 69.)

Total working days and non-productive days

Here you identify the working days, then deduct the non-productive time:

Resource Planning Model									
Team	<Team Name>								
Productive Days Calculation						Non Productive			
Employee Name Timesheet Code	Count	Days in Year	Weekends	Bank Holidays	Working Days	Annual Holiday	Sickness (Provision)	Absence	Non-Productive Total
<Employee : 25 days hol>	1	365	104	8	253	25	5	1	31
<Employee : 25 days hol>	1	365	104	8	253	25	5	1	31
<Employee : 30 days hol>	1	365	104	8	253	30	5	1	36
<Spare>		0	0	0	0	0	0	0	0
<Spare>		0	0	0	0	0	0	0	0
<Spare>		0	0	0	0	0	0	0	0
<Spare>		0	0	0	0	0	0	0	0
<Spare>		0	0	0	0	0	0	0	0
<Spare>		0	0	0	0	0	0	0	0
<Spare>		0	0	0	0	0	0	0	0
Totals	3				759	80	15	3	98

Investment days

Next you need to take into account the investment time:

Resource Planning Model									
Team	<Team Name>								
Productive Days Calculation			Non Productive	Investment					
Employee Name	Count	Working Days in Year	Total		Training	Performance Appraisals	Technology	Dept & Team Meetings	Total Investment
<Employee : 25 days hol>	1	253	31		12	2	6	2	22
<Employee : 25 days hol>	1	253	31		12	2	6	2	22
<Employee : 30 days hol>	1	253	36		12	2	6	2	22
<Spare>		0	0		0	0	0	0	0
<Spare>		0	0		0	0	0	0	0
<Spare>		0	0		0	0	0	0	0
<Spare>		0	0		0	0	0	0	0
<Spare>		0	0		0	0	0	0	0
<Spare>		0	0		0	0	0	0	0
<Spare>		0	0		0	0	0	0	0
Totals	3		98		36	6	18	6	66

Productive days calculated
Now you can determine the productive days:

Resource Planning Model							
Team	<Team Name>						
Productive Days Calculation							
Employee Name	Count	Days in Year	Working days in Year	Non Productive Total	Investment Total	Productive Days	Utilisation %
<Employee : 25 days hol>	1	365	253	31	22	200	79.05%
<Employee : 25 days hol>	1	365	253	31	22	200	79.05%
<Employee : 30 days hol>	1	365	253	36	22	195	77.08%
<Spare>		0	0	0	0	0	
<Spare>		0	0	0	0	0	
<Spare>		0	0	0	0	0	
<Spare>		0	0	0	0	0	
<Spare>		0	0	0	0	0	
<Spare>		0	0	0	0	0	
Totals	3	1095	759	98	66	595	78.39%

The consultancy model
For those of you in the consultancy business, identify the days which could be lost. (Explanation of the columns is given in the resource planning and utilisation chapter, p.69.)

The Consultancy Model Employee Name	Count	Working Days in Year	Original Productive Days	Less Travel Time	Lost Days	Non Conformance	Cancellations	Pre-Sales	Revenue Days	Utilisation %
<Employee : 25 days hol>	1	253	200	6	7	10	6	30	141	55.73%
<Employee : 25 days hol>	1	253	200	6	7	10	6	30	141	55.73%
<Employee : 30 days hol>	1	253	195	6	7	10	6	30	136	53.75%
<Spare>		0	0	0	0	0	0	0	0	
<Spare>		0	0	0	0	0	0	0	0	
<Spare>		0	0	0	0	0	0	0	0	
<Spare>		0	0	0	0	0	0	0	0	
<Spare>		0	0	0	0	0	0	0	0	
<Spare>		0	0	0	0	0	0	0	0	
Totals	3	759	595	98	0	0	0	0	418	55.07%

8. Identify the 'dummy' projects
The employee budget model gave the list of non-productive and investment projects. So, the list developed at the start of:
- new system implementation
- end-user training
- installing a single module
- troubleshooting
- upgrading systems from one release to another
- ad hoc consulting

can be added to (for example):
- holidays
- sickness
- absence
- training
- performance appraisals
- pre-sales
- dept & team meetings

and so forth.

If the holiday year and the financial year do not correspond then decide how this will be handled – is the 'holiday' project to be set up at the start of the financial year to report comparison by financial year, or set up to match the holiday year?

9. Develop the utilisation class list
This is used to map the project classification to the utilisation model. This can be either:

Primary class
Non–productive
Investment
Productive/Revenue

or could be refined further:

Primary class	Sub-class
Non–productive	Holiday
	Sickness
	Absence
Investment	Training
	Performance appraisal
	Pre-sales
Productive/Revenue	None

The purpose of the sub-class analysis is to assist in presenting the numbers. Remember that the figures for holiday, when taken across the whole organisation, will add up to a significant number. It might be more worthwhile to show the totals not by the three main classes, but with sub-class analysis on non-productive and investment with a total for revenue/productive.

10. Develop the entity list and coding structure
This is the list of items required to be stored. For example:

> programme
> project } these were identified above
> customer
> employees (who will keep timesheets) – these should be in the budget model
> cost centre
> department
> role/position
> subcontractor – these should be in the budget model

activity
capital items/inventory list
non-capital items
miscellaneous items
expense analysis
suppliers/vendors.

The list for your business may be different. This is the standing data which needs to be configured before transactions can be entered. Of course, the project and programme lists were identified earlier.

From this, deduce the coding structures. For example, what is the key for an employee, their initials, and their employee number in the payroll? How do you identify subcontractors?

The mapping of entities for the subsequent reporting needs to be defined now. Recall from the budgeting chapter that it is recommended that the mapping of codes from budget, through to project plan, through to timesheets is consistent.

When posting data to the nominal ledger there needs to be a mapping to the account code structure for revenue and cost codes.

11. Define the employee costs

I recommended in the budgeting chapter that standard costing should be used in place of actual payroll costs.

For each of the positions/roles listed, agree with your financial director the standard cost which can be used in reporting.

12. Define the charges

In a professional services business, you need to define the charge rates. Identify if the charges are to be by the hour, by the day, or part thereof.

Will different charge rates be used by role, by activity?
What is the method of revenue recognition?
How are expenses to be recharged?

13. Identify the purchase costs

The costs for the project or programme will cover a number of areas. There are direct costs such as the purchase of capital items. Indirect costs may be charged to the programme, like a head office overhead. Nevertheless, it is important to list all the costs and where they are likely to come from.

14. Review the contract terms

Check the contract terms that are agreed with the customer. Ensure that these are consistent with the system being implemented. Subtle changes to contract terms could assist in the processing of data and bring about operational improvements. Identify if any changes can be incorporated. Be careful when selling these ideas internally. It is not a good idea to open with 'Well, it would make the system more efficient' if talking to a sales person whose interest is in closing the sale, not in the operational processing of data.

15. Define a day

What is a working day? The contract of employment for an employee could say it is '7.5 hours'. It is likely that this will vary depending on your industry. What is important, from time-recording, revenue and cost views, is to define:

- What half a day is (in hours and minutes)
- What a full day is (in hours and minutes)
- What a day and a quarter is (in hours and minutes)
- What a day and a half is (in hours and minutes)
- When overtime payments are made
- When the charge rate is changed to reflect overtime/weekend hours/bank holidays.

Note for international projects
Which days are working days? This is important for international projects where the working week may not be Monday to Friday.

16. Define the data requirements

The software requirements chapter gave details of the possible information requirements. For each of the entities identified above (programme, project, employee, etc.) list the data that is needed. For example, for a project:

Unique project ID
Project name
Customer address – for project
Customer address – for sales invoices
Project manager
Business manager
Sales manager
Estimator
Department
Purchase order number
Customer ID – in sales ledger
Customer contact
Customer project manager
Customer additional contact 1
Customer additional contact 2
Project class
User-definable fields
Project classification (user definable)
Programme – link to programme table (allows multiple links)
Order received date (from customer)

Forecast start date
Actual start date
Forecast end date
Actual end date
Working hours definition
Project status
Project location (main)
Fee structures
Template jobs
List employees who can work on the project
Comments/notes (a free text field)

17. Define the reporting requirements

Create a base set of reports for the system. For each report, check that the data is held in the system and can be extracted in a timely manner.

It is here that the cash-flow report could be created. Check with your accounts department over any preferred format. The chapter on cash explains how to do this.(See page 64.)

18. Define the outputs

The outputs from the system are items such as purchase orders, sales invoices, sales statements, project reports. These link back to reporting requirements.

In a professional services organisation, the sales invoice format can be particularly important. Ensuring that the system you use can produce invoices in the correct format is not insignificant.

Consider if email is to be used to support the invoices (for example, for project reporting). Make sure the data can be extracted by invoice number electronically. You do not want to re-key information.

19. Cultural issues

The tribal knowledge of your organisation is important to understand when implementing change. It is necessary to get senior backing for the introduction of a new system, and the review of the outputs.

If there is no timesheet culture in place, then there will be a significant learning curve and change in working habits. It might be better to capture time with only one activity on a project rather than try and introduce detailed activity analysis at the same time as timesheet capture. You will have to become a champion of time recording.

Likewise, if it is a large system to implement, consider prototyping the approach with a range of projects and a few employees.

If you are moving towards weekly reporting, then timeliness becomes a key issue. Look at the process of entering timesheets at the moment. If it is monthly then there will be a perception that more pressure (and therefore work) is being put on the project team who have to fill in timesheets at the end of each week.

20. Resistors to change

Projects and programmes are about change. List the people who you think would resist this implementation. Look at:

1. Those who would have to submit timesheets. (If they are not doing this at the moment there will be resistance to being accountable)
2. Individuals who are rewarded based on a project or programme margin. (If the margin at the moment is notional, and a more realistic figure can be derived which would negatively affect them, they will resist your changes)
3. Senior stakeholders who do not want visibility of failure. Presenting the numbers at the end of a project or programme will highlight successes and failures. Such presentation and delivery will require careful management.

21. Technological infrastructure requirement

The example user map on page 137 tells us a great deal about what access is required to the system.

In reviewing a particular package (or packages), identify what hardware, operating systems (server and PC), database software, and reporting tools will be required in addition to the package.

Conclusion

Each system will have its own particulars and ways of working. The implementation will include installation of software. Time-recording software, if it has to be installed on many PCs, will require a significant overhead just to get the software in place.

Make sure that you get the design correct. Once the data is being recorded, then the number of transactions will grow quickly. For each employee there may be more than one entry per day (for timesheets); so with 20 employees, you are collecting at least 20 entries per day.

The education of people and the timeliness of data are paramount. Before going live, check that all the components are in place.

Once the data is available for analysis, be careful when presenting it. The numbers may not be what is expected. Management of expectation and introducing improvement programmes should aid in the continuing acceptance of the system.

SOFTWARE REQUIREMENTS
Introduction

It is likely that your own organisation will have specific areas that need addressing. Revenue recognition may be straightforward. Time recording could be on a single site. There might be only one currency. With no external subcontractors, cost control is limited to purchases.

Alternatively, you might be working across multiple sites, with many currencies, using a combination of internal and external resources, contracting for materials and sourcing from many different suppliers.

So, you need to identify the key requirements when selecting a system before investigating the software marketplace.

If your requirements are complex, choose an integrated system. If you try using a time-recording system from one vendor, the sales order processing system in your accounting system to invoice the customer for non-time-related items, and a separate purchasing system, you are likely to discover that:

a. Invoice production will be difficult
b. Reporting across projects and programmes will be hard, if not impossible, to perform
c. Enforcement of business processes will only be possible through manual controls which add time and expense to the whole administrative process.

However, if your requirements are simple, and the primary issue is the recording of time, then a time-recording package might be sufficient for your needs.

The system described below is adapted from the Great Plains Project Accounting Module. This is from Microsoft Business Solutions and I am grateful to them for agreeing that I could prepare a requirements list based on their software functionality.

In the introduction to the module Microsoft state: 'The project accounting suite can be used to set up, enter and maintain project records and transactions. It is also possible to budget resources, manage purchases, schedule tasks, monitor costs, bill customers and recognise revenues.

'There are three project levels used in project accounting:

Contract: This is a group of projects that a contractor performs for a customer, and for which the contractor charges the customer for various costs. For example, the contract "marketing services" might be made up of the projects "printing brochures" and "logo design".
Project: This is a group of related tasks that, together with other projects, constitutes a contract. A project is made up of cost categories. Each project has its own budget. For example, the project "printing brochures" might be made up of the cost categories: offset printing, layout, design and typesetting.
Cost category: This is a name assigned to a project expense, for example, labour, building rental or purchase of computers. When a cost category is used in a project, it is usually called a "budget item". Each cost category that is assigned to a project has its own budget.'

Project and Programme Accounting

Requirements list presentation
The details listed below are in the form of a checklist and series of questions based around the Great Plains Project Accounting Module. This is to assist you in identifying your own requirements, and preparing a list to evaluate different supplier offerings.

Software requirements: set-up

Requirement	Available (Y/N)

Projects
Can a project be assigned the following status? –
    closed
    completed
    estimate
    on hold
    open
 	
Project types
Can a project be assigned one of the following project types? –
    cost plus
    fixed price
    time and materials
 	
Profit types
Can a project be assigned one of the following profit types? –
for time and materials
    billing rate
    mark-up %
    none
    price level
 	
for cost-plus projects
    % of actual
    % of baseline
    none
    price level
    profit/unit fixed
    profit/unit variable
    total profit
 	
for fixed-price projects
    % of baseline
    none
    price level
    profit/unit fixed
    total profit	

Requirement	Available (Y/N)

Billing and Profit types
 Can a project be assigned the billings for the following?
 time and material projects based on
     billing rate
     mark-up %
     none
     price level
 	
 billings for cost-plus projects
     % of actual
     % of baseline
     none
     price level
     profit/unit fixed
     profit/unit variable
     total profit
 	
 billings for fixed-price projects
     % of baseline
     none
     price level
     profit/unit fixed
     total profit
 	
 Revenue recognition
 Can revenue be recognised based on project or contract?
 	
 Are the following revenue recognition formulas available?
     actual cost expended
     combined earnings
     estimated cost
     percentage of project completed
     percentage of task completed
     project amount
     segmented earnings
     per cent completion of fees
 	
 Multi-currency
 Can the software handle multi-currency transactions?
 Can the software enable transactions to be viewed in their functional or originating currency?
 	
 Change orders
 Can you use change orders to track modifications to? –
     budgets
     fees
     total costs
     for a project or multiple projects	

Project and Programme Accounting

Requirement	Available (Y/N)

Users and user classes
Can a user be given a unique ID?
Can a user be linked to a user class?
Can the user be given selected access to one or more of the following?
    billing note entry
    change billing rates
    change billing types
    allow change of department
    allow change of pay code
    allow change of project status
    allow entry of new budget items.
    allow entry of new material items
    allow PO closing
    allow PO printing
    allow set closed to project costs
    allow set closed to project billings
    allow transaction postings

Projects
Can projects be defaulted in terms of the following?
    decimal places for quantities
    decimal places for currencies
    contract and project status options
    posting accounts (to the nominal ledger)

Can user-defined fields be created for the following?
    customer
    employee
    vendor
    equipment
    contract
    project
    cost category
(against each of the respective forms)

Timesheets
Timesheet security
Can the following tasks be controlled through timesheet security?
    allow period entry
    allow entry by time
    allow entry by units
    allow zero quantity
    allow zero unit costs
    exceed total budget quantity
    exceed total budget costs
    exceed total budget revenue/profit
    allow add access on the fly

Requirement	Available (Y/N)

Contract classes
 Can a contract class be set up with the following?
     unique ID
     description
     default contract billing note
     default per cent commission
 	
 billings notes for:
     timesheets
     equipment logs
     miscellaneous logs
     purchasing invoice
     employee expense
     inventory
 	
 Project class
 Can a project class be set up with the following?
     unique ID
     description
     default project billing note
 	
 billings notes for:
     timesheets
     equipment logs
     miscellaneous logs
     purchasing invoice
     employee expense
     inventory transfers
 	
 Cost category class
 Can cost category classes be set up with the following?
     unique ID
     description
     hourly pay codes
     salary pay code
     unit of measure
     unit of measure schedule
     unit cost
     profit type
     billing rate	

Requirement	Available (Y/N)
Equipment class Can equipment classes be set up with the following? 　　unique ID 　　description 　　unit of measure 　　unit cost 　　profit type 　　billing rate **Miscellaneous class** Can a miscellaneous class be set up with the following? 　　unique ID 　　description 　　unit of measure 　　profit type 　　billing rate **Customer class** Can customer classes be set up to do the following? 　　specify billing settings 　　post accounts to be used **Vendor class** Can vendor classes be set up to do the following? 　　specify purchase order format 　　specify project settings 　　specify posting accounts **Employee classes** Can employee classes be set up with the following? 　　unique ID 　　description 　　employment type (hourly/salary) 　　default pay code 　　employed by 　　overhead calculations of: 　　　　amount per unit 　　　　percentage of actual cost 　　profit type 　　billing rate **Inventory transfer set-up** Can the system be configured with: 　　next document number 　　cost description 　　default billing note from 　　price level from 　　default site ID 　　user-defined fields	

Requirement	Available (Y/N)

Employee expense set-up

Can employee expenses be initially configured with the following?

    next document number
    default billing note
    cost description
    unit cost source
    profit type source
    default payment method
    user-defined fields
    tax calculation method

Purchase order set-up

Can purchase orders be initially configured with, and to allow, the following?

    next document number
    different format types
    allow zero quantity
    allow zero unit cost
    exceed total budget quantity
    exceed total budget cost
    allow hold/remove hold of purchase orders

Purchase invoice set-up

Can purchase invoices be initially configured with, and to allow, the following?

    next receipt number
    cost description default
    allowed % variance from purchase order unit costs
    user-defined prompts
    multi-currency decimal places

Purchase invoice security set-up

Can the following security profiles be set up?

    override document number
    allow zero quantity
    allow zero cost
    exceed total budget quantity
    exceed total budget costs
    exceed total budget revenue/profit
    exceed total PO quantity
    exceed total PO costs
    exceed PO unit cost
    allow receiving without a purchase order

Requirement	Available (Y/N)
Billing and revenue recognition	
When configuring the billing and revenue recognition part of the system can you do the following?	
Define next document number to be used to track transaction	
Indicate whether the quantity will be automatically adjusted when a write up or write down is entered for a billable item when performing time and materials billing	
Specify where billing discounts will be based (contract/customer/project)	
Specify whether billings will be applied first to budget or to fees	
Configure user-definable fields	
Configure billing reports	
Configure billing formats	
Define summary and detail reports such as:	
T&M consulting projects	
T&M consulting contracts	
T&M detailed projects	
T&M detailed contracts	
T&M pre-billing worksheets	
Define summary levels by:	
cost category	
cost category class	
cost category + cost owner	
cost owner	
cost owner class	
cost owner + cost category	
cost owner + cost category class	
cost owner + document number	
date + cost owner + cost category	
position (employee)	
position + rate	
Print all transaction detail	
Print all line items summarised into a single line	
Billing and revenue recognition security	
Does the system allow you to set up security on billing?	
Does the system allow you to set up security on revenue recognition?	

Requirement	Available (Y/N)
Posting accounts Can posting accounts be set up (to post data into the main ledgers) for the following? *Time and material accounts* 　　　work in progress 　　　cost of goods sold/expense 　　　contra account for costs 　　　unbilled accounts receivable 　　　unbilled project revenue 　　　accounts receivable 　　　project revenue/sales *Fixed price/cost plus accounts* 　　　work in progress 　　　contra account 　　　accounts receivable 　　　project billings 　　　project expenses 　　　project revenue 　　　project losses	

Requirement	Available (Y/N)
Multi-currency management	
When setting up for multi-currency can you define the following?	
currency ID	
description	
currency symbol	
symbol before amount	
symbol after amount	
include a space	
separator format for decimals	
separator format for thousands	
negative sign	
display negative sign before amount	
display negative sign after amount	
When setting up exchange rates can you define the following?	
exchange rate tables	
exchange rate source	
rate frequency	
rate variance	
rate calculation method as multiply or divide	
transaction rate default on exact date/previous date/next date	
search for unexpired rates as unlimited or limited	
Can you set up posting accounts for the currencies based on the following?	
realised gain	
realised loss	
unrealised gain	
unrealised loss	
financial offset	
sales offset	
purchasing offset	
rounding write-off	
rounding difference	

Software requirements: standing data

In the Great Plains Project Accounting module, standing data is created in an option known as 'cards'. The field lists given below relate to the data which is stored against cards.

Requirement	Available (Y/N)
Contracts	
customer ID	
customer name (look up from sales ledger)	
contract ID	
contract name	
contact number	
contract status	
class ID	
contract manager	
business manager	
address ID	
purchase order number	
user-defined fields	
begin date	
end date	
closed to project costs	
closed to billings	
define a default accounting method	
Change orders	
Can the contract be configured for change orders with the following?	
next change order number	
tracking of change orders	
tracking of change orders for new budget add on the fly	
Contract billing settings	
Can the system be configured for specifying billings settings for the following?	
sales person ID	
territory ID	
per cent commission	
per cent commission applied to billings only or contract total	
discount per cent	
tax address ID	
default billing format	
billing cycle ID	
revenue recognition cycle ID	

Project and Programme Accounting

Requirement	Available (Y/N)

Vendor records
 (Vendor records will come from the accounts payable system)
 Can the system be specified for vendors in terms of the following?
     default PO format to use
     unit of measure
     unit cost
     profit type (for T&M)
     billing rate (for T&M)
     profit type (for cost plus)
     per cent of baseline (for cost plus)
     profit type (for fixed price)
     total profit (for fixed price)
 	
 Employee records
 The employee options window is used to specify an employee's employer. This information is used whenever the employee is used in records and transactions.
 Can you create employee records with the following?
     employee ID
     employee name
     employed by
     default pay code
     employment type (hourly/salary)
     unit of measure
     unit cost
     project manager (yes or no)
     business manager (yes or no)
     overhead calculation as
         amount per unit
         percentage of actual cost
     profit type (for T&M)
     billing rate (for T&M)
     profit type (for cost plus)
     per cent of baseline (for cost plus)
     profit type (for fixed price)
     total profit (for fixed price)
     user-defined fields	

Requirement	Available (Y/N)
Cost categories	

Cost categories represent the individual budget items in a project. Cost categories need to be created then be assigned to the projects which are being tracked.

Can you create cost category records with the following?
- cost category ID
- category name
- class ID
- hourly pay code
- salary pay code
- unit of measure
- unit of measure schedule
- unit cost
- profit type (for T&M)
- billing rate (for T&M)
- profit type (for cost plus)
- per cent of baseline (for cost plus)
- profit type (for fixed price)
- per cent of baseline (for fixed price)
- tax option
- user-defined fields

Can you set up overheads for cost categories containing the following?
- amount per unit
- percentage of actual cost

Project and Programme Accounting

Requirement	Available (Y/N)

Project records
Projects are assigned to contracts.
For each project you create can you store the following?
    customer ID
    contract number
    project ID
    project name
    status
    project class ID
    project manager ID
    business manager ID
    estimator
    department
    purchase order number
    accounting method
    customer contact
    default billing type
    begin date
    end date
    user-defined fields
    closed to project costs
    closed to billings
Can you define fees according to the following?
    % of baseline cost
    % of baseline revenues
    lump sum
Can you define frequency of fee according to the following?
    scheduled
    per invoice
    at project completion

Project fee budgets
Can you create separate budget items?
For each budget item can you create a budget by year?
For each budget year, can you break the year into periods with baseline amounts per period?

Rate tables
Can you create schedules of cost and profit formulas for when manpower and equipment are utilized in projects?
Can you assign cost categories to a project?
Does the cost category contain the following?
    category code
    begin date
    end date
    status
    total cost (unit cost * quantity plus overhead cost)
    transaction where used (employee expenses, equipment logs, miscellaneous logs, purchases/materials, timesheets)
    unit of measure
    unit cost

Requirement	Available (Y/N)

Cost category budgets
 Can you create cost category budgets holding the following?
     category ID
     category name
     status (open or completed)
     billing note
     forecast begin date
     forecast end date
     actual begin date
     actual end date
 	
 Can you create forecasts for cost category budgets?
 Can you create an overhead button for cost categories containing
     overhead calculation as either amount or unit or per cent of actual cost?
 	
 Can you assign a rate table to a cost category?
 Can you assign inventory items to a cost category?
 Can you create a position rate table (for computing pay whenever an employee with a particular position is deployed in a project)?
 	
 Can you create an employee rate table containing the following?
     employee ID
     pay code
     hourly rate
     profit type
     overhead amount
     overhead %
     profit amount
     profit %
 	
 Can you create an equipment rate table containing the following?
     equipment ID
     hourly rate
     profit type
     profit amount
     profit %	

Project and Programme Accounting

Requirement	Available (Y/N)

Equipment records

Can you create equipment records for a project containing the following?
- equipment ID
- equipment name
- class ID
- unit of measure
- unit cost
- profit type – time & materials
- billing rate – time & materials
- profit type – cost plus
- per cent of baseline – cost plus
- profit type – fixed price
- profit/unit – fixed price
- user-defined fields

Change orders

Can you create change order records to amend a contract or project containing:
- contract number
- change order number
- change order date
- track changes to baseline or forecast
- description
- customer change order number
- change order status
- requested by
- estimated by
- approved by
- position of approver
- approval date
- begin date
- end date
- revised by
- position
- reason for revision
- last revised date
- status (pending/unapproved/approved/cancelled/completed)

Can change orders be flagged by type of: internal/company/customer?

Can the budget be revised storing the following?
- initial quote amount
- quoted prepared by
- final quote amount
- quote approved by
- quoted approved date

Requirement	Available (Y/N)

Miscellaneous records
Can you create records of miscellaneous items which hold the following?
- miscellaneous ID
- name
- class ID
- unit of measure
- unit cost
- profit type – time & materials
- billing rate – time & materials
- profit type – cost plus
- per cent of baseline – cost plus
- profit type – fixed price
- profit/unit – fixed price
- user-defined fields

Fees
Can you create fees which you can assign to projects?
Can fee types be specified as the following?
- project fee
- retainer
- retention
- service

Can the fee entry contain the following?
- fee ID
- name
- fee amount as a value
- begin date
- end date
- user-defined fields
- frequency

Billing cycles and revenue recognition
Can you create a billing cycle record which holds the following?
- cycle ID
- description
- frequency
- billing date
- cut-off date

Can you define transactions to include the following?
- timesheets
- equipment logs
- miscellaneous logs
- purchase invoices
- employee expenses
- inventory

Requirement	Available (Y/N)
Templates	
Can you create templates to assist in data entry?	
Can templates be created for the following?	
contracts	
billing settings for a contract	
project	
billing settings for a project	
cost categories	
budgets	
overheads for a budget	
assign rate tables to a budget	
assign inventory items to a budget template	
a fee template	
an access list template	
an equipment list template	
Buyer records	
Can you create buyer ID records?	

Software requirements: transactions

Transactions are posted against:

- timesheets
- employee expenses
- equipment logs
- miscellaneous logs
- inventory transfer
- purchase order
- receivings
- purchasing invoice
- billing
- revenue recognition
- series posting and project closing.

These are detailed below.

Requirement	Available (Y/N)
Timesheets	
Can timesheets be posted in batches?	
When entering timesheets can you store the following?	
employee ID	
period begin	
period end	
currency ID	
reporting period	
date of work	
project number	
cost category ID	
time begin	
time end	
quantity	
bill type	
unit of measure	
unit cost	
pay code	
department	
position	
total cost	

Requirement	Available (Y/N)
Expenses	
Can expenses be posted in batches?	
When entering expenses can you store the following?	
employee ID	
start date	
end date	
date of expense	
project reference	
cost category ID	
description	
billing type	
quantity	
unit of measure	
unit cost	
purchases total	
taxes	
Can expenses be separated out between personal expense and reimbursable expense?	
Equipment log transactions	
Can equipment log transactions be entered to record the cost of utilizing equipment in projects?	
Can equipment log transactions store the following?	
equipment ID	
reporting period	
period begin	
period end	
date	
project number	
cost category ID	
time begin	
time end	
quantity	
billing type	
unit of measure	
unit cost	
total cost	

Requirement	Available (Y/N)

Miscellaneous log transactions
 Can miscellaneous log transactions be entered?
 Can you enter these in batches?
 Can the system store the following?
    miscellaneous ID
    reporting period
    period begin
    period end
    date
    project number
    cost category ID
    quantity
    bill type
    unit of measure
    unit cost
    total cost
 	
 Inventory transfer transactions
 Can inventory transfer transactions be entered?
 Can you enter these in batches?
 Can the system store the following?
    project number
    cost category ID
    item number
    unit of measure
    quantity
    unit cost
    type
    description
    price level
    mark-up %
    billing rate
    site ID
    serial number
    lot numbers	

Requirement	Available (Y/N)
Purchase order transactions	
Does the project accounting module come with full purchase order to purchase invoice receipt capabilities?	
Purchase order entry	
Can the purchase order have a combination of new and cancelled lines?	
Can the purchase order be placed on hold?	
Can the purchase order be deleted or voiced if not unposted shipment or invoice receipt exists?	
Can the purchase order hold the following?	
purchase order type	
purchase order number	
buyer ID	
date of purchase order	
currency ID	
vendor ID	
PO format (allowing different format types)	
trade discount	
freight charges	
Can each line on the purchase order hold the following?	
project number	
cost category ID	
item	
quantity ordered	
site ID	
unit of measure	
quantity cancelled	
unit cost	
extended cost	
Can you create drop-ship purchase orders?	
Can you enter additional vendor information concerning the following?	
purchase address ID (linking to a look-up table)	
bill to address ID (linking to a lookup table)	
ship to address ID (linking to a look-up table)	
shipping method (linking to a look-up table)	
tax schedule ID (linking to a look-up table)	
payment terms	
tax registration number	
confirm with	

Requirement	Available (Y/N)

Can you enter additional purchase order information against a line item of the following?
- tax option
- tax schedule ID (linking to a look-up table)
- tax amount
- inventory account (linking to the nominal ledger)
- vendor item code
- required by date
- release by date
- released date
- vendor promise date
- vendor promise ship date
- free on board of none/origin/destination

Printing purchase orders
Can you print purchase orders with different formats?
Can you print purchase orders based on different currencies?

Receiving transactions
Can you record items and their invoices in the same window if they are received at the same time?
Can you record the following? (in addition to the original purchase order)
- quantity shipped
- quantity invoiced
- tax amount
- previously shipped amount
- previously invoiced amount
- payment terms
- payment methods of
- cash
- cheque
- credit card
- term discount taken
- EU Intrastat marking

Can you record EU Instrat details of the following?
- tax registration
- country code (linking to a look-up table)
- transport mode (linking to a look-up table)
- transaction nature (linking to a look-up table)
- value basis (linking to a look-up table)
- process type (linking to a look-up table)
- tax commodity code (linking to a look-up table)
- net unit mass
- supplementary units
- trader's reference
- line mass

Can you enter shipment invoices without originating purchase orders?
Can you enter serial numbers for a purchase receipt?
Can the serial number entry be manual or automatic?

Requirement	Available (Y/N)
Can you automatically receive all open line items in a purchase order?	
Can you receive items in multiple purchase orders?	
Can you modify the invoice distribution (to the nominal accounts)?	
Purchase invoice transactions	
Can purchase invoices be entered in batches?	
Can purchase invoices be entered with the following?	
vendor document number	
vendor ID (linking to accounts payable)	
comment	
invoice date	
currency ID (if multi-currency)	
tax schedule	
PO number	
quantity invoiced	
trade discount	
freight charge	
miscellaneous charge	
tax amounts	
Can you enter additional purchase invoice information of the following?	
PO number	
project number	
cost category ID	
item	
unit of measure	
quantity invoiced	
unit cost	
match to shipment	
extended cost	
tax options	
Can you automatically post an invoice against selected purchase orders?	
Can you modify an invoice account distribution?	

Requirement	Available (Y/N)
Billing transactions	

Can you create billing batches?

Can you create billing transactions containing header information of the following?
- invoice number
- date
- customer ID
- name of person to send invoice to
- customer PO number
- bill to address ID (linking to a look-up table)
- comment
- cut-off date
- currency ID

Can you enter detail information of the following?
- project number (ie, multiple projects per invoice)
- type (T&M, fixed price etc)
- fee amount
- trade discount
- retention amount
- project name
- tax schedule ID (linking to a look-up table)
- tax amount
- project total billing amount
- project PO number
- billing commission amount

Can you amend the distributions for the posting accounts?

For time and materials billing can you create transactions which contain the following?
- date
- cost owner
- cost category ID
- current quantity
- current amount
- current billing rate
- current mark-up %
- invoice write up/write down amount
- invoice write up/write down %
- invoice quantity
- invoice amount
- invoice billing rate
- invoice mark-up %
- invoice trade amount
- invoice type
- invoice billing rate
- invoice mark-up %

Can you create a time and materials billing return (for T&M items that have been erroneously posted and invoiced)?

Can you perform progress billings?

Requirement	Available (Y/N)

Can progress billing transactions be created which contain the following?
- document number
- cut-off date
- project number
- project name
- customer ID (linking to customer table)
- customer name
- cost category ID
- % completed
- amount earned
- amount previously billed
- amount earned this period
- billing amount
- total cost
- accounting method
- trade amount
- tax schedule ID
- tax amount
- retention amount

Can you enter additional billing taxes and other charge information of the following?
- freight charges
- miscellaneous charges
- shipping method
- terms discount taken

Can you create commission entries of the following?
- commission amount (to a sales person)
- commission billing amount (the contract sale amount on which the sales person commission will be based)
- commission per cent
- per cent of billing

Can you perform cycle billing?

Project payments

Can you apply credit memos, cash receipt and returns to individual projects?

For project payments can you create transactions which store
- project to apply to the following?
- amount remaining
- cost category apply amount
- free apply amount
- applied amount
- applied retainer
- total billing
- discount/advances
- write off apply amount

Requirement	Available (Y/N)

Ageing billed accounts
 Can you run ageing billed accounts by customer by project?
 Can you run ageing work in progress accounts reports?
 	
 Revenue recognition transactions
 Can you calculate earnings based on the computation methods of: the following?
 	
 Segmented: % if completion = actual cost/forecast cost
 (where actual cost is the actual cost for a cost category and forecast cost is the forecast cost for that particular cost category).
 Revenue earned from cost category = % of completion * project amount.
 	
 Combined from project: % of completion = actual cost/forecast cost of project
 (where actual cost is the total cost of all the cost categories included in the project, and forecast cast of project is the forecast total cost for that particular project).
 Revenue earned from project = % of completion * project amount.
 	
 Combined from contract: % of completion = actual cost/forecast cost of contract
 (where actual cost is the total cost of all the cost categories included in the projects covered by the contract).
 Revenue earned from contract= % of completion * contract amount
 	
 Can you create revenue recognition batches?
 Can you enter in revenue recognition transactions based on the different project revenue and cost types?
 Can you enter in revenue recognition transactions based on cost categories?
 Can you perform cycle revenue recognition?
 Can you perform cycle revenue recognition based on the following?
     contract
     customer
     project	

Requirement	Available (Y/N)

Enquiries
Can you enquire on the following record types?
    revenue, profit and cost
    timesheet
    equipment log
    miscellaneous log
    employee expense
    inventory transfer
    purchase order inquiries
    billing and revenue recognition
    contract record
    project record
    equipment and miscellaneous records
    cost category
    combined history
 	
Reporting
Can you create reports as follows?
    project accounting report summary
    set-up reports
    purchasing analysis reports
    billing activity reports
    posting journals
    history reports
    analysis reports
    performance reports
    utilisation reports	

Requirement	Available (Y/N)

Can you print lists as follows?
    contract class list
    contract list
    contract template list
    cost category class list
    cost category list
    customer list
    employee-based rates
    employee class list
    employee list
    equipment assignment list
    equipment class list
    equipment rates
    fees list
    job title rates
    labour assignment list
    miscellaneous class list
    overhead list by customer
    overhead list for all
    project list
    project template list
    unit of measure schedule
    user class list
    vendor class list
    vendor list
 	
Can you print purchase analysis reports as follows?
    expected shipments
    PO line items to release
    purchase order analysis
    purchase order status
    received/not invoiced
    shipment/invoice matching
 	
Can you print billing activity reports as follows?
    aged work in progress
    fee list – project
    invoice register
    pre-billing worksheet – CP/FP
    pre-billing worksheet – TM
    retention – customer
    retention – project
    work in progress	

Requirement	Available (Y/N)

Can you print posting journal reports as follows?
    billing report
    employee expense
    equipment log
    inventory transfer
    miscellaneous log
    purchasing invoice
    receivings
    revenue recognition
    timesheets	

Can you print history reports as follows?
    employee expense
    equipment log
    inventory transfer
    miscellaneous log
    purchase order
    purchase invoice
    receivings
    timesheets	

Can you print analysis reports as follows?
    cash budget
    earned-value analysis
    statement	

Can you print performance reports as follows?
    contracts completed
    contracts in progress
    contracts in progress by customer
    earnings from contract
    net write-downs
    projects in progress – cost category
    projects in progress – customer	

Can you print utilisation reports as follows?
    annual employee utilisation
    annual utilisation by department
    annual utilisation by job title
    monthly employee utilisation
    monthly utilisation by department
    monthly utilisation by job title
    YTD employee utilisation
    YTD utilisation by department
    YTD utilisation by job title	

Requirement	Available (Y/N)
Report destinations and formats Can you create the following file formats for the reports? 　　　　tab-delimited 　　　　comma-delimited 　　　　text file 　　　　HTML file 　　　　Adobe PDF file	

CONCLUSION

The challenge facing any organisation is to control programme and project costs, reporting actual costs, expected costs and understanding variations which have taken place.

By being able to look across multiple programmes and projects, it is possible to improve the maturity of estimating and accounting. An holistic view can be taken in resolving common issues. Management effort will then be focused on improving systems, processes and training, which should improve the organisation's maturity in programme and project delivery.

Without a structured, comprehensive design to bringing project planning together with accounting, there will be a disparity preventing, or at a minimum severely limiting, the ability to report in such a way.

This book:
- brings together the themes of programme management and project management with revenue and cost accounting;
- gives guidance on the design of the relationships and systems to obtain a better return on programme and project investment;
- provides a better understanding of revenue and cost accounting, data collection, process flows and reporting in a project or programme environment;
- lists the software and system requirements to consider when implementing a solution.

Section Five: Additional reading

BIBLIOGRAPHY

A Guide to Programme Management, OGC, ISBN 0-11-30600-8★
Against the Gods: The Remarkable Story of Risk, Peter Bernstein, ISBN 0671576461
'Core Competencies: The Core Competence of the Corporation', C. K. Prahalad, Gary Hamel, *Harvard Business Review* on audio.
Cost and Effect: Using Integrated Cost Systems to Drive Profitability and Performance, Robert S. Kaplan, Robin Cooper, ISBN 87584-788-9
Data Modelling, Business Systems Development with SSADM, OGC, ISBN 0-11-330871-X★
Managing Industrial Risk, John Woodhouse, ISBN 041247590-1
Managing Successful Programmes, 1st Edition, OGC, ISBN 0-11-330016-6★
Managing Successful Projects with PRINCE2, OGC, ISBN 0-11-330855-8★
Microsoft Clip Art
Principle Centered Leadership, Stephen Covey, ISBN 068485841X
Programme Management Demystified, Geoff Reiss, E & F Spon, ISBN 0419213503
The Effective Executive, Peter F. Drucker, Butterworth Heinemann
The Psychology of Selling, Brian Tracy, Audio Program, Nightingale Conant
The Secret of Power Negotiation, Roger Dawson, Audio Program, Nightingale Conant
The Seven Habits of Highly Successful People, Stephen Covey, ISBN 0684858398

CONTACTS

Project and Programme Accounting	John Chapman, tel: 0705 010 8617
Project Manager Today Publications	www.pmtoday.co.uk
ProgM - The Programme Management special interest group of the Association for Project Management	www.e-programme.com

If you would like to discuss any of the concepts in this book, please telephone the author on the number above.

★ References and quotations from *A Guide to Programme Management; Data Modelling, Business Systems Development with SSADM; Managing Successful Programmes;* and *Managing Successful Projects with PRINCE2* are all Crown copyright and are reproduced with the permission of the Controller of HMSO and the Queen's Printer for Scotland.

INDEX

Absence, 70, 71
Accounting period, 2
Activity, 23, 32, 33, 96
Administration time, 72
Advanced design concepts, 91
Against the gods, 123
Aged debtor report, 52
Aged debtors, 51, 52
Annual package, 37
Asset register, 30
Auditors, 46, 52, 54
Automobile Association, 86,

Bank account, 60,
Benefits, 8, 14
Board of directors, 1, 17, 19, 20
Bonus, 78
Budget, budgeting, 2, 28, 29
Business life cycle, 111

Cancellation time, 108
Capital, 23, 28, 29, 30, 43, 49, 135
Capitalised, 31
Cash management, 47
Cash, 3, 12, 16, 61, 64, 68
Cash-flow forecast, 18, 62, 64
Chancellor, 52
Change control, 13, 16, 18, 17, 19, 20, 82, 102, 103, 104
Change management, 1
Change programme, 6
Christmas 107, 112
Citrix, 62
Commitment accounting, 60
Commitment ledger, 59, 60
Commitments, 129
Company budget 28
Company meetings, 71
Company strategy, 27
Company, 96
Complaints, 109
Complex relationships, 91

Consultant, 12, 28
Contingency, 42, 43, 45
Contract, 18, 105
Core competencies, 12
Cost & effect, 126
Cost centre, 2, 28, 96
Cost plus contract, 67
Cost, 28, 102
Credit control 50, 58
Credit note, 55, 56
Credit, 47, 55
Cross charge, 82
Customer, 2, 12, 16, 17, 19, 20, 22, 23, 25, 46, 48, 61, 126, 129, 136

Data model, 133
Dawson, Roger, 44, 45, 52
Days, 40
Days, 7
Daytimer, 76, 76
Debtor, 25, 46, 52, 102
Deliverable, 48
Department meetings, 71
Deposit, 105, 106
Depreciation, 30
Design, 15, 91
Director, 47, 96
Discount, 14
Drucker, Peter, 77, 82
Dun and Bradstreet, 47

Easter, 111
EEC, 56
Effective Executive, The, 77, 82
Efficiency , 10
Employee utilisation, 6, 12
Employee, 17, 19, 20, 95, 129
Entity relationship diagram, 21, 28, 32
Entity relationship, 20
Entity, 21, 93
E-procurement, 59
Estimate, 31
Excusitis, 78
Expenses, 11, 18, 29 30, 39, 42, 49, 67, 77, 85, 135

Index

Facilitator objectives, 73
Finance director, 31, 40
Financial year, 5
France, 69

General ledger, 46, 57, 60
Germany, 69
Grants, 56
Gross margin, 112

Hardware, 23
Help desk, 99
HM Revenue and Customs, 52, 67
HM Treasury, 31
Holidays, 70

Implementing a strategy, 125
Internal management benefits, 10
Internet surfing, 83
Inventory, 100
Invoice (sales), 12, 47, 50, 51, 58, 61, 65
Invoicing, 48, 105
IT department, 3, 25, 39, 43, 61, 70
IT help desk, 112
IT services 61, 70, 85

Job costing, 1

Law of large numbers, 123
List price, 14
Lord Kelvin, 1
Loss, 55

Management accounts, 1
Manager, 96
Managing industrial risk, 73
Managing Successful Programmes, 4, 8, 42
Managing Successful Projects with PRINCE2, 43, 50, 65
Manufacturing cycle effectiveness, 11, 126
Margin, 61
Matched funding, 56
Materials, 15,
Microsoft Excel, 31, 51, 67, 128
Microsoft Project, 43, 50, 65

181

Middle East, 69
Miscellaneous, 30
Money, 40
Motivator, 77

National insurance, 38
Net profit, 55
Nominal ledger, 46, 57
Non-capital, 29, 30, 31, 49, 135
Non-conformance, 10, 109
Non-productive days, 7

Office of Government Commerce, 6, 8
Operational improvements, 10, 11
Order book, 49
Overheads, 16, 17, 18
Overtime, 11

P11D, 88
Parkinson's Law, 43
Payables, 59, 64
PAYE, 15, 29, 30, 41, 135
Payment terms, 65
Payroll, 18, 17, 19, 20, 28, 67
People, 15
Performance appraisal, 71
Pivot table, 128
Plucked from the air (PFA), 108
Portfolio management, 44
Pre-sales, 107
PRINCE2, 32, 37, 42, 62, 100, 105, 106
Producer objectives, 73
Producer objectives, 73
Productive days, 32, 48
Professional qualifications, 96
Profit and loss account, 29, 53, 54, 65
Profit-related pay, 37
Profit, 67, 86
Programme accounting, 1, 15, 27
Programme Management Demystified, 4
Programme, 132
Project accounting, 1, 15, 27
Project board, 17, 19, 20, 42, 136
Project budget, 28

Project initiation, 33
Project manager, 17, 58
Project sponsor, 17
Project start-up, 17, 20
Project, 2, 96, 132
Public holidays, 69
Public limited company, Plc, 70
Public sector, 1
Purchase invoice register, 60
Purchase invoice, 59, 62
Purchase ledger, 59
Purchase order, 59, 60, 62
Purchases, 17
Purchasing controls, 62
Purchasing department, 60

Quickbooks, 7

Receivables, 46, 64
Recover at cost, 86
Recover with mark-up, 86, 87
Relationships, 20, 22, 35
Repeaters, 4, 5, 62, 132
Requisition, 59,
Resource planning, 69, 107, 116, 120
Resource, 23, 290
Return on investment (ROI), 1
Revenue recognition, 32, 41, 53, 54
Revenue, 9, 17, 28, 102
Role, 96
Runners, 4, 5, 62, 132

Salary, 37, 78
Sales ledger, 46
Sales order processing (SOP), 48, 49
Sales, 17
Service fee, 54
Shareholder value, 1
Sickness, 70
Skills, 96
Software, 23
SQL, 55
SSADM, 21
Standard cost, 32, 39, 41

Stock, 100
Stopwatch, 81
Strangers, 4, 5, 62, 132
Strategic review, 13
Subcontractor, 13, 15, 17, 19, 20, 28, 29, 41, 56, 62, 135
Supplier, 17, 19, 20 32, 129

Technology, 71
Time recording, 33, 60, 72, 75, 78
Time, 17, 18, 20, 29, 30, 31, 35, 49, 129, 135
Timeliness, 37
Timesheets, 11, 15, 16, 18, 48, 60, 62, 75, 76
Tolerance, 42, 45
TOTO, 74
Tracy, Brian, 51
Training company, 98
Training, 70, 71
Travel time, 75, 107, 108
Turnover, 13

UK Government, 31
User locations, 100, 137
Utilisation, 56, 69, 107, 110, 117, 118, 120

Value billing, 115
VAT, 45, 46, 52, 67, 130

Warranties, 54
WIIFM, 76
Woodhouse, John, 73, 74
Work, 31
Working days, 7, 31, 32, 72
Working year, 69

Project Manager Today
PUBLICATIONS

Project Manager Today Publications specialises in books and journals related to project management. Titles include:

- *Managing Programmes of Business Change*
- *Managing Risk for Projects and Programmes*
- *Managing Smaller Projects*
- *One Project Too Many*
- *Right First & Every Time*
- *The Programme & Project Support Office Handbook* vol's 1 & 2
- *Using PRINCE2 The Project Manager's Guide*

and the flagship monthly magazine:
- *Project Manager Today*

Publisher of
- *Project Control Professional*

on behalf of The Association of Cost Engineers

Full details from:
Project Manager Today Publications
Unit 12, Moor Place Farm
Plough Lane
Bramshill
Hook
Hampshire
RG27 0RF

Tel: 0118 932 6665
Fax: 0118 932 6663
Email: info@projectmanagertoday.co.uk
Website: www.pmtoday.co.uk

Project Manager Today also organises topical conferences and seminars.